COMPASS

A Teaching Resource For The 11-14+ Age Group

Written by: Chris Allen, Jo Horn & Andrew Smith
Drama Scripts by: Andrew Smith
Edited by: Chris Allen

PATHFINDERS

Pathfinders (11-14 year olds) is part of the Church Pastoral Aid Society.

Making the most of...
COMPASS

THE AIM OF COMPASS
COMPASS aims to help you make disciples of the members of your group. Disciples are learners, so you are helping the young people learn about Jesus and what it means to follow Him. Each session contains a selection of material for you to choose from. This means that you can choose the ideas and activities that are most appropriate for the young people in your group and vary the way you present material week by week.

WHAT IS LEARNING?

1 Understanding
Young people need to understand Christian truth. That truth is found in the bible. There is nothing boring or irrelevant about the bible. It is our educational methods that are often out of date and need attention. COMPASS will help you teach the bible in a manner that will be appealing to your young people, and help them to understand Christian truth.

2 Remembering
It is no good teaching your young people Christian truth if they are going to forget it! COMPASS helps your young people remember what they learn. "Learning off by heart" has become unpopular. COMPASS encourages you to learn a verse of scripture each session. Never learn this together as a group with all the young people repeating the verse aloud, or they will equate this activity with kindergarten! Always learn in pairs, as if you were trying to remember some complicated physics formula. Bear in mind that the seed of Scripture you plant now might not bear fruit for many years.

How you communicate with your young people will determine how much they remember.

☞ **HEARING**
This is simply you talking and them listening! Always choose your words carefully, and make sure what you say is succinct and to the point.

☞ **SEEING**
This means adding visual aids to back up what you say. If you have the first ten books of COMPASS you will have quite a stock pictures you can adapt and use in your sessions. The leaders' resource pages often contain illustrations to back up the teaching content.

☞ **DOING**
This means involving the young people in activities, and is the principle way in which young people remember the truths you are teaching them. Activities take time, but it is well invested time. Learning one thing well is better than learning ten things that will soon be forgotten. COMPASS draws on many activities used regularly in secular education.

☞ **TELLING**
Young people of this age are now becoming quite capable of telling others what they have learnt. COMPASS encourages you to put your young people into pairs and small groups so that they can put what they have learnt into their own words.

3 Practising
Understanding and remembering Christian truth is a waste of time unless it is put into practice. COMPASS uses drama, rôle play and allegories in particular to enable the young people to apply the teaching to their everyday experience. Always be ready to tell your young people what it means to be obedient to a particular piece of teaching.

IF YOU'RE NEW TO COMPASS...
The first ten books of COMPASS explain more fully the different features of this particular teaching syllabus. If you ever have any comments, criticisms or queries please don't hesitate to contact us at the Pathfinder office either in writing or on the 'phone. It's always good to hear from you.

Making the most of...
THE BIBLE

THE GREAT UNKNOWN

For most young people the bible is totally unknown. You can't even assume that young people know the most famous stories. This does **not** mean that you leave the bible alone, but make it the most central part of your sessions, presenting the readings from it as interestingly as possible. Have confidence in it. Don't apologize for using it, but create an air of anticipation every time you are about to open its covers! The Scripture Union video "How to Beat the System" aims to smash the idea that the bible is boring, out of date and irrelevant.

GO FOR IT!

Communicating the message of the bible lies at the heart of COMPASS. The teaching content hardly ever tells you specifically to read through the main passage being used. It assumes that you will. There are many ways of reading through the passage as a group. Vary the way you do the reading each week, making sure that the method you use doesn't detract from the reading itself.

WARNING!!!

Some of the young people in your group may not be able to read aloud very well. This can be a painful and embarrassing experience for them. Aim to ask the group members in advance of the session if the passage is more than a couple of verses. Always give them the freedom to say "No", but always feel free to ask them again on another occasion.

USE REFERENCES AND PAGE NUMBERS

Make sure that the group members understand what **2 Timothy 3:16** means (ie the second book of Timothy, chapter three, verse sixteen). It's worth learning it once you have looked it up! Aim to use a common version, preferably the Good News Bible, and give the page numbers out so that those less familiar with bible will be able to find the books easily (it saves you embarrassing your fellow leaders too!).

USE GROUP MEMBERS

Having said that some young people get very embarrassed at reading in public, many young people will enjoy reading aloud. Never allow it to become a way by which they can show off, but encourage them in this skill. It is good preparation for when they read in church. Young people often make better readers than adults because they prepare more carefully.

USE OTHERS

Some adults, though, have a particular skill in reading aloud. If there are people in your church with that skill, invite them to come to give the reading one week.

USE RESOURCES

The Dramatised Bible does a lot of the hard work for you in breaking up passages into different parts for people to read. If your church hasn't got a copy, you can easily convert a normal bible passage into a dramatic reading.

USE SPECIAL EFFECTS

Some readings lend themselves to having **sound effects** added. The reading of another passage may be enhanced by showing some **slides or cartoons** on the OHP depicting what it being read about. The action from some passages could be **mimed** as it is read. There may be an appropriate **piece of music** you know of that could be played it the background. Aim to **focus the eyes** of the group members on something as the passage is being read, even if it is only them following it in their own bibles.

USE QUIZZES

The Pathfinder Resource papers and the Pathfinder Pack contain ideas for quizzes that can be used in conjunction with the bible (eg spot the mistake, crossword, quick-fire questions, blockbusters, etc) Adapt a current TV quiz game to help you learn the bible.

Making the most of... YOURSELF

Answer this question...

What is the most valuable resource in any work with young people? If you are not sure of the answer, take a piece of silver paper and look directly at the most reflective side. What do you see? The answer to both the question and the exercise is yourself! The young people in your group will remember you many years after they have forgotten everything you ever said to them. Your life, standards, friendship, commitment, love, hospitality, etc. are what will remain in their minds as they consider what you teach them and what you claim Jesus can do in their lives. No resource, no matter how good, can take the place of the personal example, witness and love of a follower of Jesus.

Personal work

Your relationship with the members of your group is the essential backbone of all you do. COMPASS aims to help you develop that relationship as well as deepen the friendships between the group members themselves. The many activities and exercises will strengthen the way you interact with the group as you become involved in them yourself. Time spent in social activities is also well invested, along with that at meals and on trips and Ventures. Jesus spent three years living with His disciples, and so had much more time to spend with His twelve than you have with your group. Even with all that time available it seems clear from the gospels that He spent most time with Peter, James and John. He was aiming to influence them in a deep, life-changing way. Which two or three young people in your group will be different in ten years' time because of their contact with you now?

Training

This is not a popular word because is sounds like hard work, and implies that we don't know everything! COMPASS aims to train you as a leader as you use it. It will help you discover how to communicate with young people as well as giving you hints and tips about working with 11-14 year olds as you go along.

In addition to this, Pathfinders produces **Resource Papers** to help you in your work, as well as a regular mailing called the **Pathfinder Pack**. If you are not affiliated and would like to find out more details, turn to the inside back cover of this book. Pathfinders also runs **Training Events** in conjunction with the other specialized age-group sections within CPAS. For details of the current training programme, contact Pathfinders' central office. Pathfinders and the other youth and children's sections at CPAS also produce another publication which will help you in your work. It's called **Team Talk**. It is designed for use when a team of leaders get together whether it be within one specific age group or across the whole spectrum of youth and children's work within your church.

Personal Growth

It's not just the group members who need to be growing spiritually. All Christians need to be growing and learning, but most especially those who have others in their spiritual care. COMPASS aims to help you grow as a Christian, particularly by helping you to understand the bible more deeply. The introductory page for each session contains some notes on the main bible passage, and recommends further reading which will help you think through the issues more deeply. The DIGGING DEEPER part in each session is also useful for you to use in your own private study as you apply the lessons from the session to your own life before applying them to the lives of your group members.

Be Encouraged!

The more you know, the more you realize how much there is still to learn! Each leader will be well aware of the areas of weakness in his or her life. There is something wrong if that is not the case. Don't allow that to discourage you, but grasp hold of the fact that God has chosen you to work in this particular area of ministry in His church. Weakness is no problem to Him because His strength shines through it **(2 Corinthians 12:9).**

DID GOD PLAN JESUS' DEATH?

UNIT 25.1

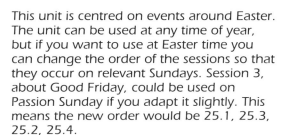

GETTING READY...

This unit is centred on events around Easter. The unit can be used at any time of year, but if you want to use at Easter time you can change the order of the sessions so that they occur on relevant Sundays. Session 3, about Good Friday, could be used on Passion Sunday if you adapt it slightly. This means the new order would be 25.1, 25.3, 25.2, 25.4.

Spend some time reading through **Isaiah 52:13-53:12**. The words may well be very familiar to you, but try not to rush through the passage. Note down the ways in which you can see Jesus fulfilling this passage. What have you got to be thankful for? During the course of the passage the concept of the Servant being punished for our sins is mentioned ten times (**verses 4-6, 8, 11, 12**).

The writer is clearly immersed in the Levitical system of sacrifice (**Leviticus: 4 & 5**). The sinful man must sacrifice a spotless lamb in order to be "at one" with God (at-one-ment). The great change here is that the Servant doesn't look for another to sacrifice, but offers Himself. The Levitical sacrificial system was a pattern of all that Jesus would do on the cross.

In the same way that Isaiah repeatedly emphasizes that this punishment was on our behalf, you cannot repeat this idea enough times so that it sinks deep into the minds of your group members. The theme will come out in each of the first three sessions of this unit.

In the gospels Jesus is clearly conscious of the road He is on. He is willing to be sent this way by His Father. Although dumb, like a lamb or sheep prepared for shearing or sacrifice, He knew all that He was doing, and why He was doing it.

The prophetic style of writing in the past tense about events that are to happen in the future is used in this chapter. This style was used in order to underline the certainty of these events coming to pass.

BIBLE PASSAGES...

Isaiah 52:13-53:12 (page 716 GNB)
see also:
1 Peter 2:22-25 (page 291 GNB)

FURTHER READING FOR LEADERS...

"**Songs of the Servant**" by Henri Blocher (IVP) pages 56-79.

FOR GROUP MEMBERS...

"**Look into the Bible**" (SU) page 60.

AVA MATERIAL...

"**The Champion**" (SU) - a series of six short episodes based around the last week of Jesus' life.

DRAMA...

"**Ced & the Wasp**" (part 5) could be turned into a short sketch.
"**Which side of the Cross?**" from 'Scene One' (Kingsway) No performance licence fee.
"**The Light of the World**" from Time to Act (Hodder). £10 performance licence fee.
See also under unit 25.3

SONGS...

For this purpose **LP 39 / SF3 364 (110)**
From Heaven You came **LP 40 / SF3 368 (120)**
God forgave my sin **FS 101 / MP 60 / SF3 369 (126)**
I have been crucified **SF2 211 (192)**
Led like a Lamb **LP 105 / MP 282 / SF2 239 (307)**
The price is paid **LP 206/SF3 497 (528)**
There is a Redeemer **LP 207 / SF3 499 (534)**
You laid aside Your majesty **LP 230 / SF3 527 (638)**

Key:
FS	Fresh Sounds
LP	Let's Praise
MP	Mission / Pathfinder Praise
SF1/2/3	Songs of Fellowship 1/2/3
( )	SF Integrated Music Edition

PRAYER...

Focus on thanking God for providing an answer to sin, and on thanking Jesus for being willing to pay the price.

CLUBNIGHT/PROJECT...

Over the next few weeks make some collages or banners which are based on some of the main events of Holy Week to make a display in the Church. You can save them for the right time if you are using this material at another time of year.

UNIT 25.1

SESSION DATE:

That the members of the group would understand that the death of Jesus wasn't a tragic accident, but necessary and planned by God.

LEADER'S CHECKLIST:

- [ ] Pens/Pencils/Paper (Parts 1, 4 & 6)
- [ ] Worksheets (Part 3)
- [ ] Illustrations (Part 5)
- [ ] Pot, Newspaper & Hammer (Part 6)
- [ ] Match up cards (Part 8)
- [ ] OHP/Visual Aid Board
- [ ] Bibles
- [ ] Song Books
- [ ] Blutac
- [ ] Notices

TEACHING CONTENT

TIME ALLOWANCE

1. CHAOS

10-15

Have the room in a state of total chaos as the young people arrive (or at least more chaotic than normal!). Make them stand over on one side as you rush around seeming to be very busy but actually getting nowhere. Ask them to arrange the room as they want it. When the room is ready, remain in a state of chaos, being unsure of what you should be doing, having lost your notes, etc. Choose a song to sing by shouting out numbers at random, and then turning to see what they are. Either abandon singing as a bad idea, or sing "There is a Redeemer" or another well known song that implies that Jesus' death was planned. Focus on the words "Thank you O my Father for giving us your Son". Lead in prayer by saying "Thank you Father that nothing You ever did was by accident. You even planned the death of Your own Son so that we could be forgiven".

INPUT FROM LEADER
Ask the group what it felt like to see everything in chaos. They may reply "normal"!
Introduce the idea of planning to them, explaining that over the next few sessions you

are going to be thinking about the death and resurrection of Jesus. In this session you are focusing on the fact that Jesus' death was carefully planned by God Himself.

2 DRAMATIZED READING   `5-10`

Read **Isaiah 52:13-53:12** in dramatic form. Share out the passage between three people. One person reads **52:13b-15** and **53:10b-12**. Another person reads **53:1b-9**. The third person has a very small part, acting as the narrator. Reading the passage through this way makes it easier to understand who is speaking, and in particular what God is saying. As a means of encouraging the young people look more closely at the passage, you could ask the group members to design a "Wanted" poster that details the kind of person the Suffering Servant was (allow extra time in your planning for this).

INPUT FROM LEADER
Although written in the past tense, these events are being described about 700 years before Jesus was born. This person was at the centre of the thoughts of many Jewish people and their religious leaders. As we will see during this unit and the next, the people failed to recognize Jesus as this Servant when He came along.

3 BEARINGS   `10-15`

Give a copy of the worksheet to every group member, explaining carefully what they must do. Allow them about three minutes for this stage. Then match them up with a partner. This could be a moment to mix the natural groupings, by putting together those who don't normally get on. Allow up to five minutes for the pairs to discuss their orders of importance and come to a solution they are both happy with.

NOTE TO LEADER
You can add atmosphere to exercises such as this one by playing appropriate music, or displaying pictures on the OHP screen. There is a space picture that can be adapted on page 37 of book 4. Rush them along because time is of the essence!

INPUT FROM LEADER
Share some of the things that are at the top of the lists. Point out that because there is no atmosphere on the moon, it would be impossible to light a fire or transmit sound signals. The moon doesn't have any magnetic poles, which renders the compass useless. Focus on the phrase at the bottom of the sheet. In the same way that careful planning might save your life in a situation such as this, God's careful planning has made eternal life possible for all of us. Look at **Isaiah 53**, reading through the whole chapter if you didn't do part 2, otherwise focusing on **verse 10**. The suffering of Jesus was the will of God so that forgiveness and life would be possible.

4 MAKE MY DAY!   `15-20`

Go into groups of three or four for this exercise. One member of each of the groups must leave the room while the other members put together a fictional time table of how that member spent the previous day from 9am until 9pm. In order to make the exercise easier, the day can be split into six 2 hour periods, and activities thought of for each of those periods. After five minutes that group member must try to discover the time-table that was created for him by asking a series of questions demanding the answer "Yes" or "No".

NOTE TO LEADER
Stay together if you have a very small group, allowing the group to think through how you spent the previous day.

INPUT FROM LEADER
When you are describing or writing about something that has already happened it is only natural to write in the past tense. All these things have taken place. Read through all, or part, of **Isaiah 53:1-12**. Although this passage describes Jesus, and is written

about 700 years before He was born, it is written in the past tense. Ask the group why they think that is. Explain that some people keep a diary of what they do, and write down each night what they have done during the day. Get them to imagine that they are writing up their diary a day in advance, because they know they won't have time the following evening. They would write it in the past tense, but they would only include things that they were really certain about doing. The reason that this prophecy is written in the past tense, is that it was so certain that it would happen, it was written as if it already had! The plans of God are certain and sure, and nothing can stop them coming into being.

5. CED AND THE WASP
5-10

Tell this story using the pictures on the leaders' resource pages, or turn it into a drama. It is based on a true story. It is a hot sunny day at school, and Cedric's class are suffering in a boring Physics lesson. All the windows are open in order to let in some fresh air. Unfortunately a wasp has also decided to come in, and is making diving raids around Cedric. He is getting fed up with this, and so he swats the wasp with his exercise book while it is in mid flight. He only stuns it though, and when the wasp recovers its senses, it decides it is going to sting the person who clobbered it. In its disorientated state though it thinks it was Cecil, who until this moment had been paying careful attention to what was being said in the lesson. The wasp was satisfied once it had exacted revenge.

INPUT FROM LEADER
This story helps us to understand what Jesus, the Suffering Servant, did on our behalf when he died on the cross. Once the wasp was hit, it became very angry, and someone was going to pay for that anger. It was the innocent Cecil who suffered and not the guilty Cedric though. In the same way the innocent Jesus suffered so that we who are guilty can avoid punishment and be forgiven. Look together at **Isaiah 53:4-6**. The punishment should be ours, but Jesus has suffered on our behalf.

> **NOTE TO LEADER**
> Alternatively, use part of the Narnia series of videos, playing to the group the scene that features the death of Aslan from "The Lion, the Witch and the Wardrobe", explaining that CS Lewis wrote the stories as an allegory of the sacrifice of Jesus on our behalf.

6. PRIZED POSSESSION
10-15

Ask the group members to write down their five most prized possessions. These should be objects of some description, and not people or animals. Then get them to number them giving number one to the most important, and number five to the least. Produce a very cheap vase, mug or glass and make up a story about it, explaining that it has great sentimental value for you. Then wrap it carefully in layers of newspaper, and smash it with a hammer. Imagine doing that to your most prized possession! You may need to explain that the story was made up and the article was of no real value at all. Ask the group now in silence to think of the person who is their most "prized possession".

INPUT FROM LEADER
It is almost impossible for us to think of allowing the person we love the most to be hurt while we just stand by and watch. How much more so to make it our wish that that person should suffer in that way for the sake of others. Look through **Isaiah 52:13-53:12** asking the group to tell you the verses that particularly highlight the suffering that God allowed His Son to endure for our sake. Draw out words and phrases such as disfigured, despised, rejected, suffering, pain, punishment, blows, treated harshly, slaughtered, put to death, sacrifice, etc.

> **NOTE TO LEADER**
> Although there are light moments in this part, you should work hard at making the group pay serious attention to what is being said. Try to learn to distinguish between fidgeting due to a lack of attention, and that caused by uneasiness as they come to terms with the seriousness and implications of what they are learning.

7. MEMORY VERSE `5-10`

In pairs learn together **Isaiah 53:11-12**. This will take longer than usual given the length of the two verses, but it is an excellent summary of what Jesus has done, and the honour He will have in the future.

8. MATCH UP `10-15`

Using the cards as on the leaders' resource pages show how accurate this prophecy was regarding all that would happen to Jesus. The cards are arranged in their correct pairings, but you need to photocopy them and cut them up. Give a set to every pair or group member, explaining that they must match up a quote from Isaiah with one from the New Testament. Take turns around the group to read the quotes out aloud.

INPUT FROM LEADER
This exercise not only demonstrates that Jesus fits the description of the Suffering Servant, but also that God was in control of all that happened to Him. Finish by focusing on **Isaiah 53:12**. Not only was God in control of all that happened, Jesus was willing to do exactly what God wanted Him to do.

9. SUMMARY

Jesus of Nazareth was an innocent man who was put to death in about 30 AD. It was no tragic accident or miscarriage of justice though. It was an event that had been planned by God since the foundation of the world, and predicted by a prophet living 700 years before Jesus was born. It was all a part of God's plan so that we might be forgiven.

10. DIGGING DEEPER

Use this part with a study or nurture group as well as making it a part of your own preparation. Look together at **Revelation 5**. The book of Revelation is not easy to understand, but some of the imagery in this chapter is straightforward and echoes the picture of a lamb being sacrificed as in Isaiah 53.

a Why did the writer cry, and what caused his tears to end?
b What in verse 5 indicates that the Lamb is Jesus?
c What was the most significant aspect of the appearance of the Lamb?
d Why is the Lamb described as worthy to open the seals?
e What did the sacrificial death achieve?
f What rôle do God's people have?
g How does this passage link in with **Isaiah 53:12**?

FOR LEADERS ONLY

Young adolescents often feel under-valued. Have you managed to convey to the group members how much value God places on them?

We despised him and rejected him. **Isaiah 53:3**	Pilate said to the people, "Here is your king!". They shouted back, "Kill him! Kill him! Crucify him!" **John 19:14-15**
He endured suffering and pain. **Isaiah 53:3**	Pilate had Jesus whipped…the soldiers made a crown of thorny branches and placed it on his head…they spat at him. **Matthew 27:26-30**
He was treated harshly, but endured it humbly; he never said a word. **Isaiah 53:7**	Jesus kept quiet and would not say a word. **Mark 14:61**
He was arrested. **Isaiah 53:8**	The Jewish guards arrested Jesus. **John 18:12**
He was lead out to die. **Isaiah 53:8**	They led him out to crucify him. **Mark 15:20**
No one cared about his fate. **Isaiah 53:8**	A servant girl said "This man was with Jesus!". But Peter denied it, "Woman, I don't even know him". **Luke 22:56-57**
He was buried with the rich. **Isaiah 53:9**	There came a rich man from Arimathea, named Joseph, who took the body and placed it in his own new tomb. **Matthew 27:57-60**
He had never committed a crime or ever told a lie. **Isaiah 53:9**	Pilate said to the chief priests and the crowds, "I find no reason to condemn this man.". **Luke 23:4**
I will give him a place of honour. **Isaiah 53:12**	…God raised him to the highest place… so all beings on earth and in the world below will fall on their knees. **Philippians 2:9**
He willingly gave his life and shared the fate of evil men. **Isaiah 53:12**	They crucified Jesus, and the two criminals, one on his right and the other on his left. **Luke 23:33**
He took the place of many sinners and prayed that they might be forgiven. **Isaiah 53:12**	Jesus said, "Forgive them, Father! They don't know what they are doing.". **Luke 23:34**

LEADERS' RESOURCE PAGES

CRASH LANDING

You are one of the crew on board a space craft which has had to crash land 200 miles from the rendezvous point with the mother ship. You are on the light side of the moon. The rough landing has damaged a lot of your equipment on board, but the items below are intact. Whether you live or die depends on you being able to reach the mother space craft. Your task is to rank the items below in order of importance, giving the number 1 to the most important item, and the number 12 to the least important. After you have done the first part on your own, you will have to compare your order or importance with that of fellow astronaut, and come to agreement.

- **20 litres of water** ☐ ☐
- **20 metres of nylon rope** ☐ ☐
- **Box of matches** ☐ ☐
- **Concentrated food** ☐ ☐
- **First-aid kit** ☐ ☐
- **Magnetic compass** ☐ ☐
- **One case of tins of dried milk** ☐ ☐
- **Portable heating unit** ☐ ☐
- **Signal flares** ☐ ☐
- **Solar powered FM two-way radio** ☐ ☐
- **Star Map** ☐ ☐
- **Two .45 calibre pistols** ☐ ☐

Careful planning makes life possible.

WHAT KIND OF KING IS JESUS?

UNIT 25.2

BIBLE PASSAGES...

Matthew 20:29-21:17 (page 29 GNB)
Zechariah 9:9 (page 924 GNB)
Philippians 1:27-2:11 (page 245 GNB)

FURTHER READING FOR LEADERS...

"**Matthew**" by RVG Tasker (IVP-Tyndale series) page 196f.

AVA MATERIAL...

"**The Champion**" (SU) - a series of six short episodes based around the last week of Jesus' life.

DRAMA...

"**A likely story!**" written by Andrew Smith especially for this session is included on the leaders' resource pages.

SONGS...

Ascribe Greatness **MP 14 / SF2 165 (18)**
For Your kingdom is coming O Lord **SF3 366 (115)**
Hosanna, hosanna, hosanna **LP 72**
Led Like a Lamb **LP 105 / MP 282 / SF2 239 (307)**
Majesty **LP 123 / MP 151 / SF2 257 (358)**
Meekness and majesty **LP 138**
Prepare the way **SF3 475 (458)**
You are the King of Glory **MP 279 / SF1 158 (630)**
You laid aside Your majesty **LP 230 / SF3 527 (638)**

Key:
- **FS** Fresh Sounds
- **HF** Hymns of Fellowship
- **HTC** Hymns for Today's Church
- **LP** Let's Praise
- **MP** Mission / Pathfinder Praise
- **SF1/2/3** Songs of Fellowship 1/2/3
- **()** SF Integrated Music Edition
- **SLW** Sounds of Living Waters

PRAYER...

Give praise to Jesus the King. Focus on **Matthew 21:15**. Even the children were shouting praise, and the religious authorities didn't like it. Remember though that these shouts of praise changed within a week. We must mean it.

CLUBNIGHT/PROJECT...

See under 25.1

GETTING READY...

Like many stories in the Bible, the events of Palm Sunday have often been popularized for children. There is clearly nothing wrong with this, but we must beware of making this only a children's story because it happens to include a donkey in it. The problem may be ours more than our group members. If they have no background knowledge of this event because they have come from a non-church background, they may have the advantage of being able to see it in a fresh way.

This is the story of God in human flesh proclaiming Himself the Messiah by riding into Jerusalem towards one of the most painful deaths ever constructed by man. Building on from the last session (or from 25.3 if you are using the alternative order) we know that Jesus was a willing participant in this drama which would pay the eternal price for sin.

Read through **Matthew 20:29-21:17** carefully as you begin to prepare. How will you be able to recapture something of the celebration of the day? We know that everything had turned around by the end of the week and the crowd had been manipulated into shouting for Jesus' death. On this day though, it was all celebration.

The session does not look at **Matthew 21:16**, which is a quote from **Psalm 8:2**. In your preparation, though, it is worth considering what insights the group members may have into Jesus that those of us who are older and wiser have missed.

The quote from **Zechariah 9:9** explains why there was the celebration, and indicates something of the high level of expectation there was in the minds of the people. For those who had eyes to see, the King was coming, albeit with a different method of achieving victory than had originally been envisaged. Pray that the group members will recognize Jesus, and accept Him as their King.

UNIT 25.2

WHAT KIND OF KING IS JESUS?

aim

SESSION DATE:

To help the group members understand that Jesus is the king who had been promised to the Jews for hundreds of years, but His kingdom is personal and not political.

LEADER'S CHECKLIST:

- [ ] Green paper, sellotape, balloons etc (Part 1)
- [ ] Video, TV, and player (Part 1)
- [ ] Biographies (Part 2)
- [ ] Pens/Pencils/Paper (Part 3)
- [ ] Disguised objects (Part 4)
- [ ] Sketch & props (Part 6)
- [ ] Jigsaw on paper/acetate (Part 7)
- [ ] Worksheets (Part 8)
- [ ] OHP/Visual Aid Board
- [ ] Bibles
- [ ] Song Books
- [ ] Blutac
- [ ] Notices

TEACHING CONTENT

TIME ALLOWANCE

1. CELEBRATION

10-15

There was a great mood of celebration on the day that Jesus rode into Jerusalem on a donkey. Decorate your room as if you are welcoming someone home. Make some paper palm branches by rolling up some green A4 pieces of paper along the longest side. Sellotape one end and about 3 inches up from that end. Then tear strips back to where the higher piece of sellotape is. Sing a couple of lively songs and wave the "branches" at appropriate moments. Let off a few party poppers, and design some balloons to fit into the occasion. As you read through the passage listed below, encourage the group to shout out the words of the crowd. Read those verses a couple of times, waving branches, letting off poppers etc.

16

If possible, show the clip of Jesus riding into Jerusalem on Franco Zeffirelli's "Jesus of Nazareth". The entry into Jerusalem is featured on part 3 of the video. Many local video hire shops stock it. Allow extra time in your planning for showing it.

INPUT FROM LEADER
Read through **Matthew 20:29-21:17** together. There was a great mood of celebration in Jerusalem because the people thought that Jesus was coming to take His place as King. He knew exactly what would happen though. Look back to **Matthew 20:17-19** to see how Jesus would really establish His kingdom.

2 BIOGRAPHIES
5-10

Bring along to the group a selection of biographies of famous people who are now dead. Ask the group to work out about what percentage of the biographies are dedicated to the last week of the person's life. How much space is given describing the person's death? How do they compare with the biographies of Jesus (ie the gospels)?

INPUT FROM LEADER
The last week of Jesus' life, and His death, are considered by his biographers to be of very great importance if we consider the amount of space that they are given. The rest of this unit will be thinking about the last week of Jesus' life, and why it was so important. In this session we are looking at the events on the first day of that week, which we celebrate on Palm Sunday.

NOTE TO LEADER
The gospel writers give the following proportions of their writings to the last week of Jesus' life - **Matthew:** eight out of twenty-eight chapters; **Mark:** six out of sixteen; **Luke:** five out of twenty-four; and **John:** nine out of twenty-one.

3 DESCENDANTS
10-15

In pairs tell the young people to describe what the world might be like in 1,000 years. Help them to focus their ideas by suggesting to them some ares they can concentrate on (eg education, home life, health care, communication, travel, etc). Write up some of their suggestions at the front. Next, ask them as a group to suggest the kind of events that have happened during the last ten years that might be remembered and talked about in one thousand years' time.

INPUT FROM LEADER
It is almost impossible to think what life would be like so far in the future because we know how much things have changed during just the past one hundred years. The world is changing more rapidly now than it has ever done. Read through the incident that happened as Jesus approached Jerusalem during the last week of His life in **Matthew 20:29-34**. Notice the title that they used of Jesus. They called Him the "Son of David". King David had been alive 28 generations (about 1,000 years) before Jesus. He had been the greatest king in the history of Israel, and the people knew that the king who had been promised to them would be one of his descendants (see also **Matthew 21:9, 15**). When the blind men had been healed they joined the crowd who were marching with Jesus into Jerusalem. Everyone thought Jesus was coming to Jerusalem to be crowned king. He knew that the only crown He would wear would be made of thorns.

4 DISGUISED OBJECTS
10-15

Before the session starts wrap up about ten objects, disguising some, and making others more obvious. If you're feeling extravagant buy some cheap wrapping paper, otherwise newspaper will do very adequately. Include in the ten something outlandish such as a bicycle! Number the objects, and tell the group members to write down what they think they all are.

> NOTE TO LEADER
> When running a quiz like this it is sometimes beneficial to leave the answers until after you have given your input in order to keep the attention of the group.

INPUT FROM LEADER
At Christmas time presents are sometimes put under the tree ready for Christmas day when you are allowed to open them. Sometimes it's fun to guess what the presents are before you open them. Sometimes it's a bad idea because we are disappointed when we find out what's really inside the package. Some people go to great lengths to disguise their gifts though. Read through **Matthew 21:1-5**. The fact that Jesus was riding on a donkey was a sign to the people that He was the king they had been promised years before (see **Zechariah 9:9**). He was like a present that is easy to recognize. On the other hand, though, the people were disappointed when they eventually discovered that He wasn't coming to kick out the Romans and establish political power. He was not what they hoped for.

MEMORY VERSE

`5-10`

Learn together **Matthew 21:5**, which shows that all that happened was a part of God's rescue plan. Encourage the group by telling them they are learning two verses at once because this verse occurs in **Zechariah 9:9**! Point out to them that in the time of Jesus a donkey was a noble animal, worthy of a king, and was a sign of peace.

A LIKELY STORY!

`5-10`

Perform the sketch on the leaders' resource pages involving the leaders or group members.

INPUT FROM LEADER
It's very easy to pass over **Matthew 21:1-3** and miss the significance of what was going on here. Two disciples were sent to take a donkey and her colt, and all they were told to say was that "The Master (or Lord) needs them". What happened was very different to what happened in the sketch, as the owner of the animals believed the disciples and let them go immediately as Jesus had prophesied. Every detail was planned so that God would keep His promises (see **verses 4-5** and **Zechariah 9:9**).

IT ALL FITS

`10-15`

Copy the jigsaw on the leaders' resource pages and cut it up. Give a piece of the jigsaw to a pair or small group of members. Give them time to write down what it says in their passage about the coming king and then piece the jigsaw back together to gain an overall picture of who the Jews were waiting for. Ask each group to summarize in a sentence what the Jews expected from the coming king.

> NOTE TO LEADER
> If you are using an overhead projector you could photocopy the page on to an acetate and then ask the group members to write directly on to the acetate so that all the group can see the picture pieced together on the screen.

INPUT FROM LEADER
From these passages we know that the king was going to be God's choice, that He would obey God, and that He would rule with wisdom and justice. His kingdom would be provided by God, and would be a kingdom of peace where the people were united under God's law for ever. The Jews were right to expect this for this is what God had promised. However, they could not see how this could be carried out if it was not by force. It had always been clear though that the promised one would come in peace, as symbolized by riding on a donkey. You will be thinking more about Jesus the Messiah in the next unit when you look at some of the titles of Jesus.

8 BEARINGS

`15-20`

Give a copy of the worksheet to every group member, telling them to work on their own or in small groups to design a T-shirt that summarizes the kind of king that Jesus was. They can either do this by drawing something appropriate, or by thinking of of a slogan that could go partly on the front, and partly on the back. Give them an example such as FRONT: Most kings wear crowns of gold - BACK: Mine wears a crown of thorns.

NOTE TO LEADER
If you live in a town you may be able to find a shop that prints T-shirts. Alternatively, the group could decide on a slogan and design which goes on the front, and then you could put the name of your group on the back.

INPUT FROM LEADER
In small groups discuss what it means for Jesus to rule in our lives. What do we have to do to show that He is in charge? How do we know what to do in order to please Him?

9 SUMMARY

The triumphal entry of Jesus into Jerusalem shows us that He is king and that He comes in peace. When Jesus comes again His kingdom will be seen by everybody. Until then, Jesus' kingdom lies in our hearts.

10 DIGGING DEEPER

Use this part with a study or nurture group as well as making it a part of your own preparation. Look at **Philippians 1:27-2:11**. Look on a map to see exactly where this church was. Paul clearly loved this church very deeply indeed, and in this passage is concerned that they persevere in their faith despite what might come their way.

a What is of prime importance according to Paul?
b Make a list of the ways in which Christians need to work together.
c What view does Paul have towards suffering?
d If we claim that Jesus is our King, what difference should it make?
e In what way is Christ's work still to be completed?
f Who will know that Jesus is King next time He comes?

FOR LEADERS ONLY

Think of one area of your own life that still needs to come under the authority of Jesus.

A LIKELY STORY

Dodgy Dave: Owner of Dave's Donkeys.
Clive & Helen: Characters looking for donkey.
Props: A sign reading "Dave's Donkeys" and a Donkey (a hobby horse or similar).

Enter Helen and Clive. They look very nervous. They approach the donkey and begin to untie it, all the time looking round anxiously.

Clive: Are you sure about this?

Helen: Yeah, it's no problem. Look he said "Go and find a donkey" and what better place than a second-hand donkey dealer.

Clive: Well that's what I mean. You have to watch out buying a second-hand donkey from Dodgy Dave. A friend of mine bought one from here that was supposed to be low mileage with one careful owner. He only got just down the road when the back leg fell off.

Helen: No, you worry too much. Look just untie this one will yer, and we'll be off.

(They untie the donkey. They then act as if it's alive, making out that they are having difficulty holding it because it's trying to escape. There are lots of cries of "whoa there Dobbin" etc. Dave hears the commotion and enters not looking at all pleased)

Dave: Can I help you?

Helen: We are just taking this donkey if that's OK?

Dave: Well funnily enough that's not OK. If you want to test ride one, then come into the office and we'll sort out the paper work.

Clive: I told you we shouldn't do this.

Helen: (To Clive) Shut-up will you? (To Dave with authority) It's alright, the boss said he wanted it.

Dave: (Very sarcastically) Oh well that's all right then. Tell you what, don't just take that one, take the others, in fact why not have the whole business if that's what the boss wants.

Clive: (To himself) We just want one that has still got four legs (Dave hears this and gives him a dirty look, Helen kicks Clive).

Helen: I told you to shut-up (To Dave) Now, you're a reasonable man. All we want is to borrow this animal for a short while, and then return him. You see our boss sent us to collect a donkey and told us to say that "he wants it". So if we could just take this then that'll be OK.

Dave: You're right; I am a reasonable man; but if you take that donkey out of this garage - I'll cut your legs off.

Clive: (To Helen) He'll do it Helen, remember the donkey.

Helen: Of course, you do realize that there will be thousands of people watching our boss ride into Scunthorpe* on your donkey (pause with Dave looking vaguely interested) think of the publicity, a thousand people watching our boss ride a donkey that has painted on the side 'This donkey was supplied by Dave's Donkeys...'

Clive: ...and still has all four legs.

Helen and Dave: Shut-up!

Dave: Well it's a nice idea, but No. If you want the donkey you'll have to buy it the same way everyone else does. Now I can do you a very nice deal on this beauty. It's got very low mileage, only one careful owner.

Clive: And several careless ones by the look of it. Oh come on Helen, he's not going to give us his donkey (they begin to walk off, Dave exits). We'll just have to think of some thing else.

Helen: Yeah, I guess you're right (pause) say, what are you like at piggy backs? (They freeze).

* Or use the name of where you live.

DESIGNER T-SHIRT

Design a T-shirt that summarizes the kind of king that Jesus was. You can either do this by drawing something appropriate, or by thinking of a slogan that could go partly on the front, and partly on the back.

"Look your king is coming to you!
He is humble and rides on a donkey"

WHY DID JESUS DIE?

UNIT 25.3

BIBLE PASSAGES...

Luke 22:66-23:56 (page 112 GNB)
Hebrews 13:11 (page 283 GNB)
Romans 4:25 (page 194 GNB)
Philippians 2:8 (page 245 GNB)
Matthew 27:54 (page 43 GNB)
Mark 15:39 (page 71 GNB)
Romans 5:1-11 (page 194 GNB)

FURTHER READING FOR LEADERS...

"The Saviour of the World" by Michael Wilcock (IVP - Bible Speaks Today series) pages 189-204.

FOR GROUP MEMBERS...

"Look into the Bible" (SU) page 90-91.
"The Bible from Scratch" by Simon Jenkins (Lion) page 112.

AVA MATERIAL...

"No 1" Joe discovers people as people when he comes to the cross for forgiveness.
"The Champion" (SU) - a series of six short episodes based around the last week of Jesus' life.
"The Stranger" (SU) - Cowboy allegory of the cross and resurrection.

DRAMA...

"Innocent" written by Andrew Smith especially for this session is included on the leaders' resource pages.
"The Centurion" from 'The Greatest Burger Ever Sold' (Monarch). £15 performance licence fee.
"The Newcomer" from 'Red Letter Days' (Hodder). £20 performance licence fee.
"Words of Death and Life" from 'Scene One'. No performance licence fee.

SONGS...

Beneath the Cross of Jesus **MP 20 / HF 11 (36)**
For this purpose **LP 39 / SF3 364 (110)**
From Heaven You came **LP 40 / SF3 368 (120)**
Hallelujah my Father **FS 6/MP 66 SF2 202 (149)**
I cannot tell **HF 38 (185) / MP 83**
Led like a Lamb **LP 105 / MP 282 / SF2 239 (307)**
Meekness and majesty **LP 138**
The price is paid **LP 206/SF3 497 (528)**
There is a Redeemer **LP 207 / SF3 499 (534)**
You laid aside Your majesty **LP 230 / SF3 527 (638)**

Key:
- **FS** Fresh Sounds
- **HF** Hymns of Fellowship
- **LP** Let's Praise
- **MP** Mission / Pathfinder Praise
- **SF1/2/3** Songs of Fellowship 1/2/3
- **()** SF Integrated Music Edition

PRAYER...

Focus on forgiveness. Asking God for His, and forgiving each other.

CLUBNIGHT/PROJECT...

Have a cooking session making some Hot Cross Buns.

GETTING READY...

As with most of the material being covered in this unit, there is a great danger that we will treat the subject with a certain amount of contempt because we have heard it all before. As you look at the most important historical events in Christian faith, pray that yourselves and the group members may understand all that Jesus did in a new and deeper way. You will be hoping that those in the group who don't exhibit a personal faith at this time will discover the love of God. It is important that those who call themselves followers of Jesus realize the cost of the new life we enjoy.

Create some time for yourself before you start preparing for the session itself in which you can read through the whole of the story about the crucifixion without interruption. This session is based in Luke's account, and although you won't be looking at all this material, read through the whole of **Luke 22 & 23**.

Remember that the disciples didn't understand what was happening even though Jesus had foretold that He would conquer death and rise from the grave. As difficult as it is to do, try to imagine the story as they would. A crucifixion without a resurrection. Until we grasp fully the pain, suffering, humiliation and hopelessness of the crucifixion we will not know the joy of resurrection.

Don't be worried about leaving the group members depressed at the end of the session! Those who had witnessed the crucifixion returned home beating their breasts in sorrow. They had to wait to find out the Good News. Choose the material you are going to use carefully so that you have a balance of serious items, and yet lighter moments when any tension has the chance to be released. Some young people become very embarrassed when issues are looked at very seriously. Don't be over-concerned if some seem to be trivializing the content. It may be there only way of coping with it. A lot may be sinking in.

UNIT 25.3

WHY DID JESUS DIE?

SESSION DATE:

That the group members will understand that the purpose behind the death of Jesus was to make forgiveness available for all people for all time.

LEADER'S CHECKLIST:

- [ ] Wood, hammer, nails, etc (Part 1)
- [ ] Computer paper, paints (Part 2)
- [ ] Blutac (Part 2)
- [ ] Sketches & props (Part 3)
- [ ] Acetate, water, cloth (Part 5)
- [ ] Pens/Pencils/Paper (Part 5)
- [ ] Illustration & story (Part 7)
- [ ] Worksheets (Part 8)
- [ ] OHP/Visual Aid Board
- [ ] Bibles
- [ ] Song Books
- [ ] Notices

TEACHING CONTENT

TIME ALLOWANCE

1. SYMBOLS

10-15

Collect together the symbols that we associate with Good Friday: planks of wood, hammer, 6 inch nails, thirty 10p pieces, whip, crown of thorns, piece of card reading "Jesus of Nazareth, King of the Jews", dice, sponge on a stick, vinegar, and an old curtain you can tear into two pieces. As you begin the session explain what you are going to be thinking about today. Make a rough and ready cross out of the wood as you talk, and then explain the significance of the other symbols. The coins remind us that Jesus was betrayed for 30 pieces of silver; the whip and the crown remind us of how He suffered and was mocked; the card reminds us of the charge against Him and that Pilate thought He was innocent; the hammer and the nails remind us of the agony He suffered; the dice remind us that His cloak was gambled away; the sponge and vinegar remind us of His thirst; the curtain reminds us that the barrier between mankind and God was removed.

24

NOTE TO LEADER
This should give an appropriately solemn start to the session. Even if you can't get hold of all the symbols, hammering a cross together at the beginning of the session will help focus the attention of the group.

INPUT FROM LEADER
Even the most biased reader of the story of Jesus' trial and crucifixion will admit that He was framed. Some would say that it was a terrible waste of life without meaning or purpose. Yet as we have seen already, it was the will of God so that all people for all time can have their sins forgiven and be friends with God. Read through the story of Jesus' crucifixion from **Luke 22:66-23:56**, giving different members of the group different parts. This will help them to concentrate as well as bringing the passage to life. You will need someone to read each of the following parts: narrator, the council, Jesus, Pilate, the crowd (could be everybody except Pilate and Jesus), the Jewish leaders (these can be the same people as the council), the soldiers, the first criminal, the second criminal, the army officer. If possible, assign the parts a week in advance.

2 HIGH SPEED MURAL
`20-30`

Stick up some continuous computer paper around the room and paint the sequence of events surrounding the death of Jesus. Give each group member a different episode to depict. This can either be done with paint or large felt tip pens. The pens are obviously a loss less messy. You will end up with something similar to the Bayeaux Tapestry!

NOTE TO LEADER
The time this activity will take depends on the amount of care you put into it. The time allowance is based on you only allowing up to ten minutes for each person to complete their particular section. The end result, if you limit the time, is unlikely to be fit to hang in the Louvre, but it will help the group members who are less artistic. The faster the mural is done, the less the difference between the artistic abilities of the group members will be noticeable. If you have an artistic church member, you could ask them to draw the scenes in pencil before the session, and then ask the group members to colour them in.

INPUT FROM LEADER
There is no particular input for this part. The aim is to help the young people understand the sequence of events surrounding Jesus' death. The main part the story can be found in **Luke 23:13-49**, but you could go back as far as **Luke 22:47** and as far as **Luke 24:12** if you want to include the arrest and resurrection of Jesus.

3 INNOCENT

The series of sketches on the leaders' resource pages can be done all at once, or performed at different points throughout the session. Make sure you use the final one, as that one contains the character who was willing to be accused even though he was innocent. Use the input after the final sketch.

INPUT FROM LEADER
Ask the group to identify the differences and similarities between the sketches. Look together at **Luke 23:13-25**. Both Pilate and Herod failed to find any reason for condemning Jesus. In fact their agreement brought them closer together because until now they had been enemies. Had Jesus protested His innocence or stuck up for Himself at all, He almost certainly would have been released. He allowed Himself to suffer and die because He knew it was the will of His Father. Look back to **Luke 22:42**.

4 DO YOU KNOW PETER?
`5-10`

Seat everyone in a circle for this activity. It will help focus the young people on the way that Peter denied Jesus. The person starting off (A) says the name of someone else in the group (B), and then asks the question "Do you know Peter?". B replies "No, A, I don't know Peter. C, do you know Peter?". Person C then replies "No, B, I don't know

Peter", and so on around the group. You can eliminate people as they get it wrong if you wish. You can make it more difficult by adding other rules such as not asking someone who's already been asked. Alternatively you could have a number of forfeits ready for those who get it wrong. Adapt the game according to the size of your group.

INPUT FROM LEADER
As we've already read, it wasn't people being asked whether they knew Peter, but Peter being asked if he knew Jesus. He denied this on three occasions, despite being warned that he would do this (see **Luke 22:31-34**). He was one of Jesus' closest friends. This was an indication of just how frightened he was. Look together at **Luke 22:54-62**. Ask the group members to think of times when they have denied knowing someone. What was the cause of it? Have there been times when they have denied knowing Jesus? What was the cause of it? Have there been times when our behaviour has made us look as if we aren't one of Jesus' followers? Help them realize we are all guilty of what Peter did in different ways, and need God's forgiveness.

5 SIN LIST [10-15]

Make a list of what the group would describe as "sins" on an overhead projector acetate using a non-permanent pen. Link this in with the previous part. As you are doing this, another leader needs to be making a second copy of the list without the group noticing.

> NOTE TO LEADER
> If you are on your own, make a list of sins in advance of the session. This list needs to be of a general nature so that as the suggestions are made by the group you can modify what they say in order to fit your list.

INPUT FROM LEADER
Something very strange, but very significant happened as Jesus died. Look together at **Luke 23:45**. This curtain hung between the Most Holy place in the Temple where the Covenant Box was kept, and the Holy Place where the priests could go. Only the high priest was allowed to go behind this curtain once a year. The curtain symbolized that man and God were separated. The cause of that separation is sin, and every year on the day of atonement the High Priest would make sacrifices for sin (see **Hebrews 13:11**). The tearing of the curtain signified that a perfect sacrifice for sin has now been offered.

At this point take the cloth and water and wipe out the list of sins and draw a cross on the acetate instead. Our sins can be wiped out because of Jesus' death. If we choose to go our own way and ignore all that Jesus has done, our sins remain. Put the copy of the list on the screen now. We have the choice as to whether we wish to benefit from what Jesus has done.

6 MEMORY VERSE [3-5]

In pairs learn together **Romans 4:25** in which Paul sums up the benefits of Jesus' death.

7 ST BERNARD [5-10]

Tell the story as on the leaders' resource pages, displaying a picture of the dog as you do so. If any of the group members are particularly good readers, you could give the story to them the week before to practice.

> NOTE TO LEADER
> This story links in well with the final sketch, and so it may be useful to put the two parts next to each other in the session.

INPUT FROM LEADER
In the same way that the dog died because of its obedience to its master, so Christ died because He was being obedient to his Father's will. Jesus was obedient even though He knew what it would cost. Look together at **Luke 22:41-43** and **Philippians 2:8**.

8 BEARINGS 15-20

Give a copy of the worksheet to every member of the group. A parallel is being drawn between the logic being used by those who witnessed the crucifixion, and the logic necessary in order to solve the puzzles. The answers can all be deduced by working out the pattern and counting the number of missing letters in the sequences. The answers are (1) Q; (2) W; (3) C; (4) U; (5) N; (6) G. If you want to throw another one into the mix, because they are claiming it was too easy, try this. Which is the next letter in this sequence A E F H I K L? The answer is M because it is the next letter without a curve in it!

INPUT FROM LEADER
Even those who witnessed the crucifixion and weren't followers of Jesus knew that He was very special. In **verse 48** we read the people went away in great sorrow, beating their breasts. In **verse 47** we read that even a Roman soldier recognized that Jesus was a righteous man. In other versions of this story (**Matthew 27:54 and Mark 15:39**) a Roman soldier believes that Jesus was God's Son. The most dramatic reaction to Jesus comes from one of the thieves in **verse 42**. None of these witnesses is biased, and each came to a conclusion about Jesus. What conclusions did the group members come to?

9 SUMMARY

Jesus was obedient to the will of His Father in heaven. He endured mocking, rejection and agony as He suffered the humiliation of death on a cross alongside two thieves. His death means that all the wrong things we do can be forgiven. We need to decide what reaction we have to Him. Are we going to reject Him in the same way the Jewish leaders did? Are we going to be too cowardly to do what we know to be right in the same way that Pilate did? Or are we going to come to Him as sinners needing His forgiveness in the same way as the thief on the cross? The choice is ours.

10 DIGGING DEEPER

Use this part with a study or nurture group as well as making it a part of your own preparation. Look together at **Romans 5:1-11**.

a What is the result of being friends with God?
b What can we look forward to now and in the world to come?
c According to verse 6, what did we have to do before Christ died for us.
d How do we know that God loves us?
e What has put us right with God?
f How does Paul describe our change of relationship with God?
g What reaction should we have to all that God has done?

FOR LEADERS ONLY

How often do we take for granted all that Christ has done for us? Take time to read slowly through story of the crucifixion.

INNOCENT

Mr Corpusty: HEADMASTER AT ST COLDITZ BOARDING SCHOOL
Glossop, Belper & Crudwell: PUPILS AT ST COLDITZ BOARDING SCHOOL

1 MR CORPUSTY IS SAT AT A DESK

Corpusty: (SHOUTING) Belper, I will see you now (ENTER BELPER) Now then Belper, I'm sure you know why I've asked you to come here?
Belper: No sir.
Corpusty: What do you mean "no". I should have thought that even to someone of your limited intelligence it would be obvious why you've had to come to see me again.
Belper: No, I'm afraid not Mr Corpusty, sir.
Corpusty: I see, and does it give you a clue if I say "cabbage!"?
Belper: I'm sorry sir?
Corpusty: Cabbage, boy, cabbage! You left some of your cabbage at lunch-time today.
Belper: But I didn't have any cabbage!
Corpusty: That's got nothing to do with it boy. Not eating your cabbage is a serious offence here at St Colditz school. You will therefore receive the full punishment. Six of the best (HE REACHES FOR HIS CANE).
Belper: But that's not fair! I have sandwiches! (THEY FREEZE AS BELPER IS LOOKING WORRIED AND MR CORPUSTY IS FLEXING HIS CANE AND LOOKING MALICIOUS).

2 MR CORPUSTY IS SAT AT HIS DESK

Corpusty: (SHOUTING) Crudwell, I will see you now. (ENTER CRUDWELL) Now then Crudwell, I'm sure you know why I've asked you to come here?
Crudwell: No Sir.
Corpusty: What do you mean "no". I should have thought that even to someone of your limited intelligence it would be obvious why you've had to come to see me again.
Crudwell: No I'm afraid not Mr Corpusty, sir.
Corpusty: I see, and does it give you a clue if I say "Turnip!"?
Belper: I'm sorry sir?
Corpusty: Turnip, boy, turnip! Yesterday you attacked the school eel collection with a turnip.
Crudwell: That wasn't me sir, it was Trantlebeg.
Corpusty: Trantlebeg, how dare you slander that fine boy!
Crudwell: But everyone saw him do it!
Corpusty: Well he very sensibly came and told me that you had done it, and that he had tried to save the eels.
Crudwell: Save them? He ate them!
Corpusty: Aaah what sacrifice that boy made. Well here at St Colditz School we take attacking eels with a turnip very seriously. So you will get the punishment. Six of the best.
Crudwell: But it can't have been me. I wasn't here yesterday. (THEY FREEZE AS CRUDWELL IS LOOKING WORRIED AND MR CORPUSTY IS FLEXING HIS CANE AND LOOKING MALICIOUS).

3 MR CORPUSTY IS SAT AT HIS DESK

Corpusty: (SHOUTING) Glossop, I will see you now. (ENTER GLOSSOP) Now then Glossop, I'm sure you know why I've asked you to come here?
Glossop: No Sir.
Corpusty: What do you mean "no". I should have thought that even to someone of your limited intelligence it would be obvious why you've had to come to see me again.
Glossop: No I'm afraid not Mr Corpusty, sir.
Corpusty: I see, and does it give you a clue if I say "Cup Cake!"?
Glossop: I'm sorry sir?
Corpusty: Cup cake, boy, cup cake! You force fed the school stick insect 23 cup cakes (PAUSE) Well don't you have anything to say for yourself? (PAUSE) What nothing at all? (PAUSE) Aren't you going to scream and fight like the others? Because I know you didn't do it. Trantlebeg came and told me you did, and he always lies. (PAUSE) Still not going to say anything. Right then, let's get this over with. (THEY FREEZE WITH GLOSSOP LOOKING CALM AND MR CORPUSTY FLEXING HIS CANE AND LOOKING CONFUSED).

ST BERNARD

This isn't a story about a great saint in the church from years ago, but about a dog!

In Switzerland one day, a man set off for a long walk up a mountain. He took his St Bernard with him for company, and looked forward to enjoying the scenery around him. However, while he was at the top of the mountain the weather closed in and the fog came down. The man and his dog soon got lost, and walked aimlessly around for ages, trying to find their path.

It got later and later, and then, to add to their troubles, the snow began to fall. Silently, the snow began to settle and the layer got thicker and thicker. The man was getting more and more tired, and eventually he could walk no further. He lay down to rest. As it got dark the temperature dropped, and the cold, combined with his tiredness, caused the man to begin to lose consciousness. His dog, who had always been obedient to his master, stayed as close to him as possible. As he felt his master growing colder and colder, he moved to lie on top of him. Unfortunately, his master, in his delirium, thought he was being attacked by a wolf, and drew out his knife and stabbed his dog to death.

The next morning, a rescue team set off to look for them when it was noticed they had failed to return home. They found the man with his dog lying dead on top of him. The man was alive, though still unconscious. The warmth of his dog's body had kept him from freezing to death.

LOGICAL CONCLUSION

Use your logic in order to come to the right conclusions as you solve the puzzles below. Fill the missing letter into the gap in each one. If you get stuck, write out an alphabet to help you see the sequences more easily.

1.
C	G	K
G	M	N
K	S	

2.
A	F	K
J	O	T
M	R	

3.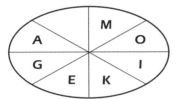

4.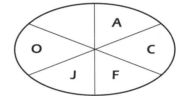

5.
Y	V	X	W
O	I	M	K
T	K	Q	

6.
H	M	I	L
U	Z	V	Y
B		C	F

Now look at **Luke 23:40-48** and identify the three sets of people who had watched all that had gone on as Jesus was crucified. They had come to their own logical conclusions that there was something very special about Jesus.

1

2

3

What conclusions had they come to?

1

2

3

In the box below write down what conclusions you have come to about Jesus

DID JESUS REALLY RISE FROM THE DEAD?

UNIT 25.4

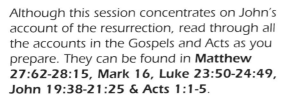

GETTING READY...

Although this session concentrates on John's account of the resurrection, read through all the accounts in the Gospels and Acts as you prepare. They can be found in **Matthew 27:62-28:15, Mark 16, Luke 23:50-24:49, John 19:38-21:25 & Acts 1:1-5**.

The Digging Deeper section also suggests that you look at Paul's teaching on the Resurrection in **1 Corinthians 15**. Note especially how Paul refers to the historical events of the Resurrection even though he is writing a number of years later to an established church. The historical facts are central and important, despite those in the church today who would say the contrary.

Note down any thing you have discovered for the first time, or anything that has come across to you in a fresh way. Once again, this will help overcome the problem of familiarity.

It is arguable that the greatest evidence for the resurrection lies in the lives of the disciples themselves. Part 8 seeks to draw this out. What about the evidence of today's disciples? Do we live lives that reflect the hope we have in Christ? What is our attitude towards death? What is our confidence about the future? As you prepare think through how the Resurrection should affect various areas of your life. Are there any situations in the lives if the group members that make this session particularly pertinent?

You will need to decide where the emphasis in the session must lie. Is your group mainly sceptical about Jesus, and therefore need convincing? On the other hand, are they seeking to follow Jesus and need their confidence in the Resurrection boosting so that they can face those who ridicule them? It may be a balance of the two, in which case you may want to meet with a few on their own who want to take these issues further.

BIBLE PASSAGES...

John 20:1-21:14 (page 145 GNB)
1 Corinthians 15 (page 716 GNB)
Acts 9:1-9 (page 161 GNB)
Acts 1:3 (page 149 GNB)
John 18:15-18/25-27 (page 142 GNB)

FURTHER READING FOR LEADERS...

"**The Resurrection - Fact or Fiction**" by Richard Bewes (Lion).
"**The Davidson Affair**" by Stuart Jackman (Faber).

FOR GROUP MEMBERS...

"**Look into the Bible**" (SU) page 90-91.

AVA MATERIAL...

"**The Champion**" (SU) - a series of six short episodes based around the last week of Jesus' life.
"**The Stranger**" (SU) - Cowboy allegory of the cross and resurrection.

DRAMA...

"**Good News**" and "**What does Easter mean to you?**" from 'Scene One' (Kingsway). No performance licence fee.
"**The Scoop**" from 'Ex Machina' (Marshall Pickering). No performance licence fee.
"**World Exclusive**" from 'Red Letter Days' (Hodder). £20 performance licence fee.

SONGS...

And Can It Be **HF 5 / LP 8 / MP 11 / SLW 85**
For this purpose LP 39 / SF3 364 (110)
From Heaven You came LP 40 / SF3 368 (120)
Hallelujah my Father FS 6/MP 66 SF2 202 (149)
I am a new creation LP 74 / SF3 384 (179)
In the tomb so cold LP 132
Majesty LP 123 / MP 151 / SF2 257 (358)
Rejoice! Rejoice! LP 169 / SF3 478 (461)
The price is paid LP 206/SF3 497 (528)
There is a Redeemer LP 207 / SF3 499 (534)

Key:
- **FS** Fresh Sounds
- **HF** Hymns of Fellowship
- **LP** Let's Praise
- **MP** Mission / Pathfinder Praise
- **SF1/2/3** Songs of Fellowship 1/2/3
- **( )** SF Integrated Music Edition
- **SLW** Sounds of Living Waters

PRAYER...

Focus on the Resurrection, and the victory won by Jesus over sin and death.

CLUBNIGHT/PROJECT...

Put together an Easter Garden that can be displayed in church (if you use this session at Easter!).

31

UNIT 25.4

DID JESUS REALLY RISE FROM THE DEAD?

SESSION DATE:

To help the group members see that the evidence points towards Jesus rising from the dead, and to encourage them to have confidence in their faith because of it.

LEADER'S CHECKLIST:

- [ ] Stove, matches, pan, eggs, etc (Part 1)
- [ ] Worksheets (Part 2)
- [ ] Identical newspapers (Part 4)
- [ ] Interview sheets (Part 5)
- [ ] Tape recorder/video camera (Part 5)
- [ ] Resurrection cards (Part 6)
- [ ] Quiz questions & prizes (Part 7)

- [ ] Pens/Pencils/Paper
- [ ] OHP/Visual Aid Board
- [ ] Bibles
- [ ] Song Books
- [ ] Blutac
- [ ] Notices

TEACHING CONTENT

TIME ALLOWANCE

1 BOIL AN EGG

10-15

As you begin the session, light up a campus gas stove and explain that you were in a bit of a rush this morning and so you missed breakfast. You are going to boil yourself an egg. Unless you think you can keep talking for the time it takes your egg to boil, it may be an idea to sing together a song about the Resurrection. When you think that your egg is done to a turn, dry it off and roll it across the table. Tell the group that it is traditional in some places to do this on Easter Day because the egg rolling across the table symbolizes the stone rolling away from the entrance to Jesus' tomb.

 NOTE TO LEADER
As an alternative you could arrange for the whole group to have breakfast together. This would be especially good to do if you are having this session on Easter Day. If

your group enjoy craft based activities, you could decorate your eggs. Allow extra time for this.

INPUT FROM LEADER
In this session we are looking at the Resurrection of Jesus from the dead. Did it really happen, or was it just a made up story? If it really did happen, then we need to decide exactly what we are going to do about it. Read through the story from **John 20:1-29**.

2 BEARINGS   15-20

Give a copy of the worksheet to every member of the group. The aim of it is to help the young people to begin to think through what evidence is convincing when we come to think about Jesus rising from the dead. You will need to explain clearly to the group that they are to note down what evidence would satisfy them as proof, rather than whether they believe something is true or not. Cut some of the categories if you are short of time.

INPUT FROM LEADER
Get some feedback about the different statements. Point out that we look for different kinds of evidence in order to establish whether things are true or not. Not all things can be proved in a scientific manner. Look together at **John 20:24-29**. Thomas was quite clear what sort of proof he was looking for. There is greater happiness, though, for those who believe in the Resurrection of Jesus without seeing Him.

3 MEMORY VERSE   3-5

In pairs learn together **John 20:29**. Encourage the group members to tell each other in their pairs how convinced they are about Jesus rising from the dead.

4 NEWS QUIZ   15-20

Divide your members into small groups and give each group a copy of a newspaper. The newspapers need to be identical. A local tabloid is ideal. The groups then divide the papers between them so that they have a couple of pages each. You ask questions which you have prepared before hand, the answers to which can be found in the papers. For example "What is Mrs so-and-so now famous for?", and "What will I be able to listen to if I tune into Radio 4 at 5.30 pm?", etc. You can make the questions as cryptic as you like.

INPUT FROM LEADER
Once you have played this game, focus in on one news item which has quotations from the people involved in it. Discuss how you know the news item is true. You could bring in ideas like it is a respectable paper and would only want to print the truth. Point out that reporters ask witnesses what they saw in order to establish the truth of a story. The Bible does the same thing. To show us that the Resurrection happened, the writers of the Gospels include accounts from people who saw Jesus after He had risen. These accounts are well detailed. Look together at **John 20:11-16** and **John 21:1-14**. The second story is particularly significant because Jesus appears to a number of people at the same time, and eats food, thus proving He was not a ghost or apparition.

5 INTERVIEWS   15-20

Go into small groups and give one of the following five passages to each small group. It doesn't matter if you give the same passage to more than one group, or if you don't use all the passages. The passages are: **John 20:11-18; 20:19-25; 20:26-29; 21:1-14; Luke 24:13-35**. Each group needs to read their passage and then draw out the facts using the interview sheets on the leaders' resource pages. They should write their answers as if they were the person being interviewed. If it is then possible to record the interviews and play them back to the whole group, then do so. It will be a different way of enabling the group members to let each other know what they have discovered in their passages. You will need to allow a lot of extra time for doing this.

NOTE TO LEADER
If you can't afford the time in the session, use an activity evening, or set up a special time for recording. If you can borrow a video camera you could turn them into TV interviews, and then possibly show them to other members of your church. Helping group members in this sort of situation gives you an opportunity to step out of the more formal teacher/pupil relationship and enables you to get to know individuals better.

INPUT FROM LEADER
Jesus appeared to quite a selection of different people in different situations. He also appeared to 500 people at one time (see **1 Corinthians 15:3-7**) and to someone who hated Christians and all he had heard about Jesus (see **Acts 9:1-9**). Saul was certainly not someone who could be accused of being a biased witness! Look together at **Acts 1:3**. Jesus spent forty days days between the time of His Resurrection and the time of His Ascension proving "beyond doubt" that He was alive.

6 WHAT HAPPENED TO THE BODY?   10-15

Use the cards on the leaders' resource pages as the basis for this activity. Split into pairs or small groups and give a set of the cards, jumbled up, to each group. They need to put the cards that are numbered 1-6 in a column. Next they look for a card that supports the theory that is on the card in the column. When they have completed that column, they need to a look for a card that will counter the arguments in the second column. They should end up with the cards in columns as laid out on the leaders' resource pages.

NOTE TO LEADER
If the group need an example to explain the method to them, give them this rather bizarre theory about how Jesus rose from the dead.
Theory: The Romans accidentally crucified Simon of Cyrene instead of Jesus.
For: Simon did carry Jesus' cross for Him.
Against: Too many people wanted Jesus dead for a mistake like that to be made.

INPUT FROM LEADER
Ask the groups if they can think of any other explanations, or any other evidence for and against the theory in the first column. There have been several people who have tried to prove that Jesus did not rise from the dead, and have failed. One was Frank Morrison who ended up writing a book called "Who moved the stone?" in support of the Resurrection. Another was Lew Wallace who ended up making the film "Ben Hur" as a witness to the fact he discovered the evidence supported the Resurrection. If you didn't use part 4, look at the bible verses listed there.

7 SECOND CHANCE   15-20

Play a favourite game with your group. It doesn't matter what it is as long as it involves giving someone a second chance if they get it wrong. If you're stuck for ideas, offer a prize to anyone who can say the memory verse exactly, including the reference. Give people a second chance if they need it. Alternatively, hold a review quiz on what you have covered throughout this unit, but again, give each team two chances at getting it right.

INPUT FROM LEADER
Remind the group of the way that Peter denied knowing Jesus on the night before He was crucified. Now look together at **John 21:15-24**. If anyone was glad to see Jesus alive again it was Peter. He must have longed for the chance to tell Jesus that he really did love Him despite what he had done. Jesus asks him three questions, corresponding to the three times that Peter denied knowing Him. Jesus makes it clear to Peter what the cost of following Him will be. Peter will be crucified (see **verses 18-19**). Peter is given a second chance, but what a second chance it is. Not only to live for Jesus, but also to die for Him.

8 WHEN WOULD YOU LIE?   `5-10`

Explain to the group that they answer the questions about telling lies you are about to give them by moving to one end of the room or another. Tell them which end of the room signifies "Always" and which end of the room signifies "Never". Putting signs on the wall with those words on at the respective ends of the room is helpful. Give an example by saying "Would you tell a lie in court under oath?". Tell them where they would need to stand in order to answer "Always", "Never", or somewhere in between. Use these questions and others of your own choosing, finishing with the final one as listed:

Would you tell a lie to protect someone's feelings?
Would you tell a lie to stop yourself getting into trouble?
Would you tell a lie to stop someone else getting into trouble?
Would you tell a lie in order to make a lot of money?
Would you tell a lie if it would cost you your life, whereas telling the truth would save it?

INPUT FROM LEADER

Reflect on how the group members reacted to the final question. It seems stupid to die for the sake of a lie, when telling the truth would let you live. In wars some people may have died in this way in order to protect fellow soldiers or secret plans. Would the followers of Jesus die for the sake of a lie? Would Peter have allowed himself to be crucified because he claimed that Jesus was risen from the dead? Given his action on the night that Jesus was arrested, it is highly unlikely. Remind the group of **John 18:15-18 & 25-27**, especially if you didn't look at it in the last session. Most of the closest followers of Jesus gave up their lives because they insisted that Jesus had risen from the dead. Look together at **Acts 12:2**. James, the brother of the writer of the gospel we have been looking at in this session, died because he insisted that Jesus had risen. Could there be stronger evidence than people being willing to be killed for their faith in the risen Jesus?

9 SUMMARY

History has shown that even those who want to disprove the Resurrection fail to do so because the strength of the evidence standing against them is so overwhelming. It seems that the gospel writers went out of their way to include the evidence of a whole range of witnesses. Jesus proved "beyond doubt" that He was alive. Being faced with the facts is one thing - doing something about them is something else.

10 DIGGING DEEPER

Use this part with a study or nurture group as well as making it a part of your own preparation. Look together at **1 Corinthians 15:1-11 & 51-58**, or the whole chapter.

a What lies at the heart of the gospel?
b How important a rôle does Paul think the witnesses of the Resurrection have?
c What does Paul mean by "By God's grace I am what I am"?
d What future hopes do we have because of the Resurrection?
e Why can the Christian laugh in the face of death?
f In what way has the Resurrection defeated death, sin and the Law?
g As we look to our future resurrection, what should we be doing?

FOR LEADERS ONLY

Beware that the problem with some group members is not that they **don't** believe in the Resurrection of Jesus, but that they **won't**! What can you do about it?

INTERVIEW INFORMATION

Name of interviewee:

Where and when did you last see Jesus?

What happened?

How did you react?

Did you recognise him straight away or when did you realise it was Jesus?

What did Jesus look like?

Did Jesus say anything to you?

What did you reply?

Did he tell you to do anything?

What did you decide to do about it?

Has the experience changed you in any way?

WHAT HAPPENED TO THE BODY?

THEORY	FOR	AGAINST
1. The Roman soldiers stole the body.	They could make money by selling the body to the followers of Jesus.	They wouldn't want to keep the popularity of Jesus alive.
2. The Jewish authorities stole the body.	They could produce the body later and prove that Jesus hadn't been raised from the dead.	They never produced the body, and they would have made themselves unclean during an important religious festival.
3. Jesus' disciples stole the body.	They could pretend that Jesus had come back to life.	They gave up their lives for the sake of what they knew to be a lie.
4. Mary had gone to the wrong tomb.	She was so overcome by grief that she didn't notice she had made a mistake.	She had followed Joseph of Arimathea when he buried the body, and she wasn't the only witness.
5. Jesus didn't die on the cross and recovered in the tomb.	There are very occasional instances in history when people who were thought to be dead have revived.	The soldiers checked Jesus was dead by piercing His side. His blood had begun to separate thus proving death.
6. Jesus had risen from the dead.	Jesus told people that He would rise on the third day, and His body was gone.	This had never happened before, and has never happened since.

LEADERS' RESOURCE PAGES

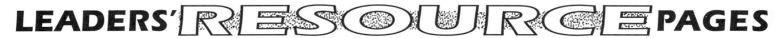

EVIDENCE

Working with others in the group, discuss what evidence you would accept to prove the truth of the statements below. Don't discuss whether the statement is true or not, but what it would take to convince you that is was true. Make a note of any statements you fail to agree on.

Pop music is horrible:

Cynthia is intelligent:

Spiders have eight legs:

There are one hundred centimetres in a metre:

Cedric will never be able to sing in tune:

Violence on television makes people more aggressive:

Jesus was raised from the dead:

WHY WAS JESUS CALLED "MESSIAH"?

GETTING READY...

The unit builds on what was in 21.2 when looking about what is special about Matthew's gospel. Each of the sessions is based in particular passages from that gospel as well as looking some of the Old Testament roots of the titles being considered. You will need to decide how well the group cope with looking at the Old Testament. This will determine how deeply you take them into the Old Testament roots. Don't ignore it altogether, though, as it is impossible to understand the way the Jews viewed Jesus without some understanding of their history.

You will also find yourself building on the sessions in the first half of this book. Try to fit the new things you are learning into the structure of the things you have already learnt. Reminding the group of what you have learnt before is not a waste of time. It reinforces the information, and helps them to build up a comprehensive picture.

It is important to make sure that in each of the sessions the young people don't just learn about Jesus in a factual way, but see the way in which they can respond if they wish to.

You will need to familiarize yourself with all the passages you are going to use in the session. As you prepare, look particularly at **Matthew 16:13-28**. In addition, read through and contrast **Isaiah 42:1-4** and Isaiah 45:1-8. The expectation was for the King Cyrus type of deliverer as in **Isaiah 45**, and not the kind of person as described in the Isaiah 42 passage.

The desire was for a military hero who would be a true "Son of David". He would be a great king, and return Israel to the days of David. King Cyrus had been the king who had delivered Israel from the Assyrians, and a parallel was seen between that occupation and the one in Jesus' time by the Roman forces. No wonder Jesus was reluctant to apply the title "Messiah" to Himself with all the misconceptions it would bring!

BIBLE PASSAGES...

Matthew 16:13-23 (page 24 GNB)
Isaiah 42:1-4 (page 703 GNB)
Isaiah 45:1-13 (page 708 GNB)
Matthew 3:13-17 (page 6 GNB)
Matthew 17:1-5 (page 24 GNB)
Micah 5:2 (page 902 GNB)
Matthew 2:1-6 (page 4 GNB)
Isaiah 9:1-9 (page 674 GNB)
Matthew 4:13-16 (page 7 GNB)
Matthew 1:17 (page 4 GNB)
Zechariah 9:9 (page 924 GNB)
Matthew 21:4-5 (page 31 GNB)

FURTHER READING FOR LEADERS...

"**Matthew**" by RVG Tasker (IVP-Tyndale series) page 156f.
If you have a Bible Dictionary of any kind, look up "Messiah" in the index.

FOR GROUP MEMBERS...

"**The Bible from Scratch**" by Simon Jenkins (Lion) page 101.

DRAMA...

"**Titles**" written by Andrew Smith especially for this session is included on the leaders' resource pages.
"**The Kept Promise**" COMPASS unit 21.2.

SONGS...

The suggestions in each session in this unit focus on who Jesus was. You could sing "You are the King of Glory" each week.
At your feet we fall **LP 10 / SF2 167 (28)**
God of Glory **LP 51 / SF2 197 (136)**
Hallelujah my Father **FS 6 / MP 66 / SF2 202 (149)**
His Name Is Wonderful **MP 72**
Jesus is King **LP 93 / SF2 236 (277)**
Jesus is Lord **MP 119 / SLW 82 / SF1 71 (278)**
Lord Jesus Christ **HF 58 (348) / LP 121**
Majesty **LP 123 / MP 151 / SF2 257 (358)**
You are the King of Glory **MP 279 / SF1 158 (630)**
You laid aside Your majesty **LP 230 / SF3 527 (638)**

Key:
- FS — Fresh Sounds
- HF — Hymns of Fellowship
- LP — Let's Praise
- MP — Mission / Pathfinder Praise
- SF1/2/3 — Songs of Fellowship 1/2/3
- ( ) — SF Integrated Music Edition
- SLW — Sounds of Living Waters

PRAYER...

Thank God that you recognize who Jesus is. Pray for friends that they might discover Him too.

CLUBNIGHT/PROJECT...

Put together a series of photo-stories based on the incidents in the main passage in each session. This involves posing and shooting photographs in black and white, and then adding speech bubbles. You can then reproduce them for the church on a photocopier.

UNIT 26.1

UNIT 26.1

WHY WAS JESUS CALLED "MESSIAH"?

SESSION DATE:

That group members would understand the meaning, significance and origins of the title "Messiah", and how only Jesus fully fitted the description.

LEADER'S CHECKLIST:

- [ ] Sketch & Props (Part 1)
- [ ] Hidden objects (Part 2)
- [ ] Profile sheets & ball (Part 3)
- [ ] Book of names (Part 4)
- [ ] Worksheets (Part 5)
- [ ] Obscure pictures (Part 6)
- [ ] Disguised characters (Part 7)

- [ ] Pens/Pencils/Paper
- [ ] OHP/Visual Aid Board
- [ ] Bibles
- [ ] Song Books
- [ ] Blutac
- [ ] Notices

TEACHING CONTENT

TIME ALLOWANCE

1 TITLES

Use the sketch on the leaders' resource pages as a way of introducing the subject of names and titles. Make the most of the pauses in order to bring out the humour. Whilst the sketch is being performed, encourage the group members to list all that they learn about the central character. After the sketch, write up at the front all you about Mr Stores. Then ask the group members to make a list of all the different ways that they might be referred to (eg full name, shortening of name, nickname, surname, etc). How do the titles we use of other people change in different circumstances (eg Mummy, Mum, Mother, Mrs Smith, etc)?

10-15

40

INPUT FROM LEADER
Names and titles can teach us a great deal about a person. We were able to put together some facts about Mr Stores. Our names give something away about us. We will call people by different names according to the situation. Jesus also had a number of titles that help us learn about Him, and over the next few sessions we are going to be looking at what these titles mean. Read out aloud **Matthew 16:13-23**. Ask the group members to tell you the four titles that are used for Jesus in the passage. They are "Messiah" (verses 16 & 20), "Son of God" (verse 16), "Lord" (verse 22), and "Son of Man" (verse 13).

2 THE CHOSEN ONE [10-15]

Before the session, hide a number of objects in your room, or outside if the weather is amenable! It doesn't matter what the objects are, but if they have a value in themselves rather than being tokens (ie mini-eggs rather than bits of paper) the hunt may be done more enthusiastically. All the objects should be of a similar nature, but one must be marked as being special (eg marked with a red cross). Give a prize to the person or pair who collect the most objects, but give a bigger prize to the person who found the special object. When you've quelled the excitement point out that although it was worth looking for all the objects there was one that was special.

INPUT FROM LEADER
The marked object was only special because it was chosen to be special. Remind the group of what you looked at in the first part of the last unit (25.1) as you looked at **Isaiah 53**. Nothing that made Jesus particularly different (**verses 2 & 3**), but He was chosen for this task by God (**verse 10**). Next look at **Isaiah 42:1-4** which makes the point that the Lord's servant was chosen (verse 1). Read together **Matthew 3:13-17** and **Matthew 17:1-5**. Ask the group to pick out the common phrase from the last three passages. Jesus is the appointed and chosen one, with whom God is well pleased. "Messiah" means "chosen one".

> NOTE TO LEADER
> You don't need many people or much room in order to have an effective hunt. This is a very adaptable activity.

3 WHO'S WHO? [15-20]

Using the personal profile sheets on the leaders' resource pages, ask each member of the group to answer the questions accurately. Make sure nobody writes their name on the sheet. Explain that the descriptions are going to be read out aloud, and the rest of the group is going to have to guess the identity of the person being described. When all the descriptions have been written, collect them in. In order to read them out, you can either ask a leader, or you may want to hand them out randomly and ask the group members to read out each other's. Choose the order of readers by throwing a ball to the first person, and then asking them to throw it to the next, etc..

> NOTE TO LEADER
> As in any activity of this nature, you will need to be sensitive to any who might see this as an opportunity to make fun of others.

INPUT FROM LEADER
We are able to identify each other from the descriptions. Some of the descriptions may have fitted several members of the group, but when you heard the whole description there was only really one person it fitted exactly. We can authenticate Jesus' claim to be the Messiah by checking the descriptions of the Messiah in the Old Testament. Compare the following pairs of passages - **Micah 5:2/Matthew 2:1-6; Isaiah 9:1-2/ Matthew 4:13-16; Isaiah 9:7-9/Matthew 1:17; Zechariah 9:9/Matthew 21:4-5**. These are only four of many very specific prophecies about the Messiah from the Old Testament that prove that Jesus was the One promised by God. The Jews don't believe that Jesus was the Messiah and that there is still someone else to come.

4 | NAMES   5-10

Most people dislike one of the names that they have. It is often a middle name. Ask the group if they are willing to say what their middle names are. Don't worry if they won't! Some people dislike their first name and use their middle name. Others hate their names so much that they change them legally. Ask the group members to think of which names they would have chosen for themselves if they could have been asked. Allow them access to a book containing the meaning of names if possible.

INPUT FROM LEADER
The title "Messiah" comes from a Hebrew word. The Old Testament is written in Hebrew, and it is the language spoken by Jews. When the word "Messiah" is translated into Greek it is the word "Christ". This title was so important it became a part of Jesus' name. He is known as "Jesus Christ", which really means "Jesus the Messiah". The word "Christ" only became a part of Jesus' name after He had returned to heaven. In fact "Christ" was a name that Jesus didn't want! Look together at **Matthew 16:13-20**. In verse 20 Jesus orders His disciples not to tell anyone that He was the Messiah (or Christ). This wasn't because He didn't like the name, but because it was misleading. The kind of messiah the Jews were expecting was an all conquering hero who would defeat the Romans. Jesus chose to use the title "Son of Man" more than any other title when He was talking about Himself. We will be thinking about that title in 26.4. "Christ" or "Messiah" was the name that Jesus kept secret until He wanted people to know exactly who He was.

5 | BEARINGS   15-20

Get the young people to work in pairs or small group on the worksheets. They must design an advert to go in the "Jerusalem Tribune" for a Messiah. They use use the top half of the sheet to work out the job description, and then design the advert to go into the box. You will need to explain to the group that they must imagine that they are living in Jerusalem under fierce and cruel regime of the Roman occupying force.

INPUT FROM LEADER
Given the military history of Israel and their plight under Roman occupation, it's not surprising that they were hoping for a Messiah who would bring deliverance from Rome. God's plan was more long term though. The Messiah would bring deliverance from sin and death. Look together at **Isaiah 45:1-8** for a description of King Cyrus. He was a "messiah" in as much he delivered the Israelites from the Babylonians and brought back the treasures to the temple. His job description may be similar to that written by the group members for their "Man Made Messiah". This is the kind of messiah the Jews were hoping for. Now look at **Matthew 16:20-21**. Jesus explains clearly how He will bring about deliverance.

> NOTE TO LEADER
> If you think that your group will struggle looking at Isaiah 45, concentrate on the passage in Matthew.

6 | WHAT IS IT?   10-15

On the leaders' resource pages you will find some pictures of some objects taken from obscure angles. Photocopy the page, and then cut it in half and give a copy to each group member. Give out the bottom half of the page to prove the answer is correct!

INPUT FROM LEADER
The exercise shows how difficult it is to identify something unless you have the whole picture. Look together at **Matthew 16:13-20**. Jesus asks the disciples two vital questions "Who do people say I am?" and "Who do you think I am?". When most people looked at Jesus they guessed He was someone important, but they hadn't got the whole picture. Simon Peter however, saw a clearer view of who Jesus was. He'd put all the pieces together and knew that Jesus was more than just a reincarnated prophet, He was in fact the Son of God - the Messiah. Jesus tells Peter that this wasn't just a good guess, but that Peter had inside information from God Himself.

7. RECOGNITION `15-20`

Cut out the pictures of some famous people from newspapers and magazines. Suitably disguise them by drawing glasses and beards on them, and then stick them up around the room. Do this to about 10 characters, and number them. Tell the group members to go around the pictures in pairs, trying to identify them.

> NOTE TO LEADER
> Remember that characters we think are famous may not be well known to the group members. It is worth buying a couple of teenage magazines especially for this exercise.

INPUT FROM LEADER
Look together at **Matthew 16:13-16**. Some people had their theories as to who Jesus might be, but only Peter truly recognized who Jesus was. He had some outside help. This was the person sent by God to save the world. His life was going to be the point of history around which everything would revolve (even our date system is based on His life). Peter needed God's help to recognize Jesus. Challenge the group to pray for God's help as they seek to understand who Jesus is, and what they must do in response.

8. MEMORY VERSE `3-5`

Go into pairs to learn **Matthew 16:16**. In this verse Simon makes two great statements that are true of Jesus. He is the Messiah and the Son of the living God. You can also use this verse as a way of previewing next session when you look at the title "Son of God".

9. SUMMARY

The Jews had been promised a Messiah for many hundreds of years. The Old Testament is full of different images of what the Messiah would be like. Some people fitted some of these descriptions, but only Jesus fitted them all. The Jews were waiting for a political leader, and so didn't recognize the Saviour that God appointed. We need to recognize Jesus as the Messiah and the Saviour of the world.

10. DIGGING DEEPER

Use this part with a study or nurture group as well as making it a part of your own preparation. Look together at **Isaiah 45:1-13** in order to grasp the parallel between Cyrus and Jesus. There are five features of the rôle of the Messiah in this passage that can be seen a part of Jesus' rôle too.

a Cyrus is the man of God's choice (verse 1).
b He is appointed to rescue and restore God's people (verses 4, 11-13).
c He is an agent of judgement on the enemies of God (verse 1, chapter 47).
d He is given authority over the nations (verses 1-3).
e In all he does he is representing God Himself (verses 1-7).

Think through the ways in which Jesus fulfils each of these five rôles.

FOR LEADERS ONLY

How do your group feel when you open up the Old Testament? What can you do to help them see it's not beyond understanding?!

TITLES

SOMEONE IS MAKING A TELEPHONE CALL AND TRYING TO TALK TO GENERAL BERTRAM CUTHBERT STORES. THE CALL CAN EITHER BE MIMED, OR A REAL TELEPHONE COULD BE USED AS A PROP IF YOU HAVE ACCESS TO ONE. IF A REAL TELEPHONE IS USED, MAKE SURE THAT THE WORDS OF THE CALLER CAN STILL BE CLEARLY HEARD.

Hello, Hello, Yes Hello is that Mr Stores? (PAUSE)
No, I'd like to speak to Mr Stores (PAUSE)
What? Yes his military title is General Stores (PAUSE)
Yes that's right General Bertram Cuthbert Stores (PAUSE)
Yes that sounds like him, Bertie Stores (PAUSE)
No, No you must have got the wrong man, he's Daphne Store's husband (PAUSE) Pardon, Old baldy bonce?!!
Well yes he does get called that sometimes (PAUSE)
OK I'll hold on (LONGER PAUSE)
Hello, (WITH OBVIOUS DISAPPOINTMENT) Oh well when will he be back then?

PERSONAL PROFILE

Don't write your name on this sheet!

Where were you born?

What's you favourite hobby?

What's your favourite food?

What's your favourite singer/group?

What's your favourite magazine?

What's your favourite colour?

Are you wearing that colour today?

What's your father's name?

What makes you most angry?

What are you frightened of?

What would you do if you had £1,000 to spend?

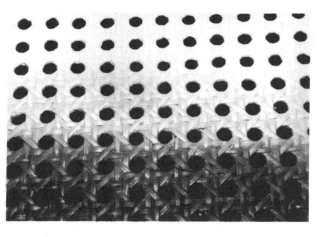

LEADERS' RESOURCE PAGES

BEARINGS

MAN MADE MESSIAH

The Jews during the time that Jesus was on earth lived under the occupation of the Roman Empire. The situation would have been similar to the time when the Iraqi occupied Kuwait. What kind of Messiah would you want if you lived under an occupying force of that kind? Work out a job description, and then design an advert which can be included in the JERUSALEM TRIBUNE.

Job Description:

Job Title:

Main tasks: 1

                2

                3

Hours of work:

Length of contract:

Answerable to:

Experience required:

Salary:

Advert:

If Jesus had applied for your job do you think He would have got it? Yes/No

What reasons do you have for not giving, or giving, Jesus the job.

IN WHAT WAY IS JESUS "SON OF GOD"?

UNIT 26.2

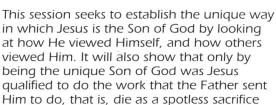

GETTING READY...

This session seeks to establish the unique way in which Jesus is the Son of God by looking at how He viewed Himself, and how others viewed Him. It will also show that only by being the unique Son of God was Jesus qualified to do the work that the Father sent Him to do, that is, die as a spotless sacrifice for sin. You will once again be able remind the group of some of the ground you covered in unit 25, as you looked at why the Father sent Jesus to die on the cross.

The session looks at a number of passages from Matthew's gospel, and at **Isaiah 9:1-7**. If you prefer to centre yourself in one passage, concentrate on **Matthew 12:33-39**. The parable of the tenants in the vineyard ties together who Jesus was with what He came to do.

Jesus is from the same place as the Old Testament prophets (ie they were called by God and Jesus comes from God). The prophets were rejected by Israel when they were alive, but by this time they were revered. Time had hidden the shameful way they were treated, and the way God's message had been ignored. Jesus is putting His finger on the hypocrisy of the religious leaders who appealed to them as a point of authority. The Pharisees realized this (verse 45) and looked for an opportunity to arrest Jesus when the crowds were not around (**Matthew 26:16**).

God has also sent His Son to the people, but he too is killed despite being God's Son, and therefore more important than the prophets. Jesus, however, foretells His future glory by quoting **Psalm 118:22-23**. The stone that was rejected by some is used by the builder for greater glory.

There are further notes about the Isaiah passage in the Digging Deeper section. Note the importance of the geography of this passage. It is the place names that confirm that the passage is talking about Jesus. It's amazing how important the smallest details of the bible can be.

BIBLE PASSAGES...

Matthew 1:18-25 (page 4 GNB)
Romans 3:21-26 (page 192 GNB)
Matthew 3:16-17 (page 6 GNB)
Matthew 17:5 (page 24 GNB)
Isaiah 9:1-7 (page 674 GNB)
Matthew 4:13-16 (page 7 GNB)
Matthew 21:33-42 (page 32 GNB)
Matthew 11:25-27 (page 16 GNB)
Matthew 15:13 (page 22 GNB)
Matthew 26:29 (page 39 GNB)

FURTHER READING FOR LEADERS...

"**Matthew**" by RVG Tasker (IVP-Tyndale series) page 203f on the parable of the Tenants in the Vineyard.

FOR GROUP MEMBERS...

"**Look into the Bible**" (SU) page 83.

AVA MATERIAL...

"**Flesh & Blood**" (SU) - a two part drama on the birth of Jesus.

DRAMA...

"**The Two Shepherds**" from 'Red Letter Days' (Hodder). £20 performance licence fee.
"**Angel Space**" from 'Lightning Sketches' (Hodder). £20 performance licence fee.

SONGS...

The suggestions in each session in this unit focus on who Jesus was. You could sing "You are the King of Glory" each week.
At your feet we fall **LP 10 / SF2 167 (28)**
God of Glory **LP 51 / SF2 197 (136)**
Hallelujah my Father **FS 6 / MP 66 / SF2 202 (149)**
His Name Is Wonderful **MP 72**
Jesus is King **LP 93 / SF2 236 (277)**
Jesus is Lord **MP 119 / SLW 82 / SF1 71 (278)**
Lord Jesus Christ **HF 58 (348) / LP 121**
Majesty **LP 123 / MP 151 / SF2 257 (358)**
You are the King of Glory **MP 279 / SF1 158 (630)**
You laid aside Your majesty **LP 230 / SF3 527 (638)**

Key:
- FS   Fresh Sounds
- HF   Hymns of Fellowship
- LP   Let's Praise
- MP   Mission / Pathfinder Praise
- SF1/2/3   Songs of Fellowship 1/2/3
- ()   SF Integrated Music Edition
- SLW   Sounds of Living Waters

PRAYER...

Jesus' job was to be the Saviour of the World. Focus your prayers on a missionary linked with your church, and on your friends who are, as yet, without faith.

CLUBNIGHT/PROJECT...

See under 26.1

UNIT 26.2

IN WHAT WAY IS JESUS "SON OF GOD"?

SESSION DATE:

That group members would understand the way in which Jesus is the unique Son of God, by looking at how He was seen by others, and what He thought of Himself.

LEADER'S CHECKLIST:

- [ ] Pens/Pencils/Paper (Part 1)
- [ ] Container (Part 1)
- [ ] Disqualification cards (Part 2)
- [ ] Paper cups (Part 4)
- [ ] Worksheets (Part 5)
- [ ] Jigsaw pictures (Part 7)
- [ ] OHP/Visual Aid Board
- [ ] Bibles
- [ ] Song Books
- [ ] Blutac
- [ ] Notices

TEACHING CONTENT

TIME ALLOWANCE

1 ELIMINATION
10-15

Ask the group members to write down one thing that makes them unique, and place it in a container. Help them by giving examples (only person with Hubert as a middle name, or only person in the group with a great aunt living in Clacton). When everyone has placed something in the container, ask the whole group to stand. Draw out of the container the pieces of paper one by one, asking the people identified to sit down (eg sit down if your middle name is Hubert). You should be left with just one person standing! It doesn't matter if several sit down at once. If you award a prize to the person left at the end it will raise anticipation as you ask everyone to stand once again. Then say "Sit down unless you are perfect". Point out the imperfections of those who remain on their feet!

INPUT FROM LEADER
Look at **Matthew 1:18-25** together. In this session you are going to be looking at why Jesus was called the "Son of God". His birth was certainly different to anyone else's, and it needed to be because of the job He had to do. He needed to be perfect. Verse 21 shows what this job was - He was to be the Saviour of the world. In order to save people from their sins He needed to be free from sin Himself. The Father of Jesus was God Himself, and so Jesus is the Son of God in a very unique way.

2 DISQUALIFICATION   10-15

Use the cards on the leaders' resource pages as the basis for a game. Either give a card to every group member and tell them to find their partner. Alternatively give a set of cards to everyone, and tell them to sort them out. The cards in outline print are meant to be things that would disqualify you from doing certain jobs. Some are technical (eg 7 and 9); most arise out of common-sense (eg 3 and 13); one is meant to be humorous (ie 8); but the most important one is number 11. Include the cards you think most useful.

INPUT FROM LEADER
If you didn't use part one, you can also use that input at this point. Each of us work at gaining qualifications that will help us to do different jobs. There are some things, though, that will disqualify us. If you are ordained in the Church of England you are not legally entitled to be a member of the House of Commons. If you have a criminal record you can't become a police officer. Other jobs may not be possible for us because of our natural abilities or handicaps. If your hands shake a lot you can't really be a brain surgeon. If you are scared of heights you'd be silly to commit yourself to spending your working life going up and down ladders. Since the time of Adam, sin had been a part of every person's nature. Every person born of human parents was automatically disqualified from being a possible Saviour of the World. Jesus is unique because His Father was God Himself. Look at **Matthew 1:20-23**. The Spirit of God caused Mary to become pregnant, and she remained a virgin until after Jesus had been born (verse 25).

> NOTE TO LEADER
> If you covered part one, or want to take this further with your group, look at **Romans 3:21-26**. All have sinned (nobody could qualify to be the Saviour of the World), but God solved the problem by sending His perfect Son, Jesus, as a sacrifice for sin.

3 CLAIM TO FAME   5-10

Try to convince your group that you are the child of someone very famous. If one of your leaders has the same surname as a celebrity all the better. If you happen to be the child of someone very famous, ask another leader to do this spoof. The group probably won't believe you, but keep pursuing the argument. Produce pictures of the famous person to try to convince them. Sound very knowledgeable about your chosen celebrity. Ask them what you would need to do to convince them. The only really convincing proof would be if this person came and admitted that all you said was true.

INPUT FROM LEADER
Jesus' claim to be the Son of God was confirmed by God Himself in the presence of many witnesses. **Matthew 3:16-17** relates what happened when Jesus was baptized. Also look at **Matthew 17:5** and what happened when Jesus was transfigured as He talked with Moses and Elijah. We can add this to the proof we looked at in the last session about how only Jesus fully fitted the Old Testament picture for the Messiah.

4 MEMORY VERSE   5-10

Encourage the group to learn **Matthew 3:16-17** in which the Father, Son and the Holy Spirit all feature. Try to make learning verses as much fun as possible. This one could be written on the bottom of paper cups, which are then filled with water (well it did take place at a river!). The group members have to drink the water, and turn the cup over.

5 BEARINGS
10-15

Give a copy of the worksheet to every group member. Encourage them to work on their own for the top half. Some of them may struggle to work out their possible earnings, but they will enjoy comparing answers. They may demand a rise when they get home!

INPUT FROM LEADER
Go into pairs or small groups as you look at **Isaiah 9:1-7**. Link verses 1-2 with **Matthew 4:13-16** which you looked at in the last session. Ask the group members what they found in the passage from Isaiah. Add to their suggestions points from the rest of that passage: He would bring the light of understanding (verse 2); He would bring great joy (verse 3); He would take away their burdens (verse 4); He would defeat their enemies (verse 4-5); He will be known as God Himself (verse 6); His power will be based on justice and will know no end (verse 7); He will be one of David's descendants (verse 7).

6 ACT IT OUT
15-20

So far in this session we have looked at how others, including the God the Father, have authenticated that Jesus was the unique Son of God. The rest of this session will be concentrating on how Jesus viewed Himself. Read through **Matthew 21:33-39**, and ask the group members to act out what they have heard read. After they have done that, read out verse 40 and ask them to dramatize what they think would have happened next.

NOTE TO LEADER
This parable contains ample opportunity for some gratuitous violence! Encourage the group to make the beatings as realistic as possible without hurting each other. The key to stage fighting lies with the person receiving the punishment. The more they react, the more it looks like they're being hurt. If you don't think your group are capable of controlling their violence, try telling the story as a series of frozen images.

INPUT FROM LEADER
The improvised endings put together by the group members may well be similar to that suggested by the people listening to Jesus tell the story. Jesus points out that their ending is only half right. The fruit of the harvest will be shared by others, but the son is not dead and gone. He turns out to be the most important of all. Jesus is clearly talking about Himself in this story. The slaves in the story represent the prophets who had been sent by God in the past. Jesus sees Himself as unique. Only He is the Son of God.

7 ODD ONE OUT
10-15

Photocopy the two pictures on the leaders' resource pages, and give a cut up copy of the top picture to each group. Mix into that a piece from the bottom picture. They should not realize immediately that there is an extra piece. You can give different pieces of the bottom picture to the different groups, and then collect them in at the end when it is realized that they are not needed for the picture of the house. Use the extra pieces to construct the picture of the palace. Award a prize to the quickest team or individual. This activity can be done as "one against one" if you have a small group.

INPUT FROM LEADER
Read together **Matthew 21:42** (or through verses 33-43 if you omitted part 6). The rejected piece, far from being worthless, turned out to be part of a much grander picture altogether. Jesus was the rejected son in the story, but turns out to be the Son of God who will reign forever (link to **Isaiah 9:6-7**).

8 LATERAL THINKING
15-20

Explain to the group that lateral thinking involves working out a solution from the facts available. A man lives on the 10th floor of a block of flats, and each morning he gets the lift as he goes to work. When he returns from work, though, he always gets out at the 7th floor and walks up the stairs for the last three flights. Why? One solution is that he is too small to reach the button to take him to the tenth floor. The second riddle is that a woman walks into a bar and asks for a glass of water. The bar man takes out a gun and fires it into the air. The woman says "Thanks" and walks out. In this case the woman was suffering from hiccups, and the shock from the gun going off got rid of them for her. After the young people have solved those riddles ask them what conclusions they would draw if someone walked into the room and claimed to be one of the richest people in the world. Encourage them towards three possible conclusions. He is either a liar, or he may be insane, or he may be telling the truth. How do we decide if he is telling the truth? By looking at what he's wearing, the car he drives, the house he lives in, etc.

INPUT FROM LEADER
Tell the group members to use the same kind of thinking as they look at **Matthew 11:25-27; 15:13; 26:29**. Who does Jesus think He is? What conclusions can we come to? As with the man who claimed to be rich, He is either a liar, or He is insane, or He is telling the truth. The writer of the Narnia stories, CS Lewis, once wrote that we cannot logically just say that Jesus was a "good man". He is either bad (a liar), or mad (insane), or God's Son (who He claims to be). As you look at all the evidence what conclusion do you come to? If you conclude He really is the Son of God, what are you going to do about it?

SUMMARY

The evidence in the bible points towards Jesus being unique. His birth was miraculous, and predicted many years before. God declared Jesus to be His Son before many witnesses. Jesus certainly thought Himself to be God's Son. He could have been lying, or possibly insane, but all the evidence of how He lived and died point towards Him being who He said He was - the Son of God.

DIGGING DEEPER

Use this part with a study or nurture group as well as making it a part of your own preparation. Have a closer look at **Isaiah 9:2-7**. Isaiah's words are directed towards King Ahaz. His words regarding Zebulun and Naphtali are particularly pertinent as those towns fell to the Assyrians within months of Isaiah's meeting with the king.

If you look back to **Isaiah 7:14** you will find details of this child's birth. If you look forward to **Isaiah 11** you will find details about his kingdom. These verses are concerned with the nature of His person, which has been the main topic of this session. "Wonderful" often means "supernatural" (eg **Judges 13:18**). Yahweh is stated as being wonderful in counsel in **Isaiah 28:29** (NIV). The title "Mighty God" is used of the Lord in **Isaiah 10:21**. "Everlasting Father" is a particularly wondrous phrase to use of a child yet to be born. "Peace" implies prosperity as well as tranquillity, which will be the nature of His kingdom or government. We now know that this was written as a prophecy about Jesus.

a In what ways does Jesus fulfil this prophecy?
b Is any part of it yet to be fulfilled?
c What security can God's people draw from this passage?

FOR LEADERS ONLY

Do we sometimes make Jesus so friendly and familiar that we lose sight of His majesty?

#	Occupation	#	Occupation	#	Occupation
1	Accountant	2	Aeroplane Pilot	3	Brain Surgeon
4	Dancer	5	Dustman	6	Electrician
7	House of Commons MP	8	Pathfinder Leader	9	Police Officer
10	Royal Navy Sailor	11	Saviour of the World	12	Singer
13	Vet	14	Vicar	15	Window Cleaner

#	Trait	#	Trait	#	Trait
1	Can't add up	2	Short-sighted	3	Shaky hands
4	No sense of rhythm	5	Bad back	6	Totally colour blind
7	Church of England minister	8	Kind, patient & forgiving	9	Criminal record
10	Can't swim	11	Imperfect	12	Tone deaf
13	Scared of animals	14	Atheist	15	Scared of Heights

LEADERS' RESOURCE PAGES

HOUSEHOLD CHORES

Look at the list of household chores below and ring the answer that is most truthful. How often do you have to...

	Daily	Weekly	Monthly	Annually	Never
Clean out pets	D	W	M	A	N
Clean the toilet	D	W	M	A	N
Clean your room	D	W	M	A	N
Cook a meal	D	W	M	A	N
Do the shopping	D	W	M	A	N
Iron your clothes	D	W	M	A	N
Make your bed	D	W	M	A	N
Mow the lawn	D	W	M	A	N
Polish your shoes	D	W	M	A	N
Set the table	D	W	M	A	N
Vacuum the house	D	W	M	A	N
Visit relations	D	W	M	A	N
Wash the car	D	W	M	A	N
Wash the windows	D	W	M	A	N
Wash-up	D	W	M	A	N

If you were given £1 for every job you did, how much would you earn in a year? Work it out by multiplying all your D's by 365, all your W's by 52, all your M's by 12, and then adding them together with all your A's.

All of us have things to do because our parents or guardians tell us to. Jesus also had things to do because He is God's Son. Look at **Isaiah 9:1-7** and make a list of some of the tasks of the Son of God. Try to find 6.

1   4

2   5

3   6

Remember that these words about God's Son were written by Isaiah many hundreds of years before Jesus was born.

WHY DO WE CALL JESUS "LORD"?

UNIT 26.3

BIBLE PASSAGES...

Psalm 110:1 (page 602 GNB)
Matthew 22:44 (page 33 GNB)
Matthew 7:21-27 (page 11 GNB)
Matthew 25:31-46 (page 38 GNB)
Acts 2:29-36 (page 152 GNB)
1 Corinthians 15:25 (page 220 GNB)
Ephesians 1:20-23 (page 240 GNB)
Hebrews 1:13 (page 273 GNB)
Hebrews 10:12-13 (page 279 GNB)

FURTHER READING FOR LEADERS...

"**Matthew**" by RVG Tasker (IVP-Tyndale series) page 81f on the two house builders.
"**Christian Counter Culture**" by John Stott (IVP-Bible Speaks Today series) page 205f

FOR GROUP MEMBERS...

"**Look into the Bible**" (SU) page 73.

DRAMA...

"**The Usurper**" written by Andrew Smith especially for this session is included on the leaders' resource pages.
"**The House on the Rock**" from 'Time to Act' (Hodder). £10 performance licence fee.

SONGS...

The suggestions in each session in this unit focus on who Jesus was. You could sing "You are the King of Glory" each week.
At your feet we fall **LP 10 / SF2 167 (28)**
God of Glory **LP 51 / SF2 197 (136)**
Hallelujah my Father **FS 6 / MP 66 / SF2 202 (149)**
His Name Is Wonderful **MP 72**
Jesus is King **LP 93 / SF2 236 (277)**
Jesus is Lord **MP 119 / SLW 82 / SF1 71 (278)**
Lord Jesus Christ **HF 58 (348) / LP 121**
Majesty **LP 123 / MP 151 / SF2 257 (358)**
You are the King of Glory **MP 279 / SF1 158 (630)**
You laid aside Your majesty **LP 230 / SF3 527 (638)**

Key:
FS	Fresh Sounds
HF	Hymns of Fellowship
LP	Let's Praise
MP	Mission / Pathfinder Praise
SF1/2/3	Songs of Fellowship 1/2/3
( )	SF Integrated Music Edition
SLW	Sounds of Living Waters

PRAYER...

God doesn't leave us alone, but gives us His Spirit to help us be obedient. In silence encourage everyone to think of one area where they need God's strength

CLUBNIGHT/PROJECT...

See under 26.1

GETTING READY...

This session centres on the need to be obedient. "Lord" is the title we use of Jesus most commonly in our prayers. Just because we call Jesus "Lord" doesn't mean that we are in a relationship with Him. It is when we treat Him as "Lord" by obeying Him that can have the assurance of salvation. The main passage we look at is **Matthew 7:21-27**.

It would very easy to get totally tied up in knots looking at this title because of the difference between the Hebrew and Greek origins! Part 2 is the only part that attempts to draw out a little of the meaning. Although you will not be using this material directly in the session, it will be helpful for you to understand more of the background. If you think that your group is able to grasp this material, use it with them.

In **Exodus 3:14** God gives Moses and the Israelites a special name to call Him. "Lord" or "I am" actually means "I am who I am, and I will be who I will be". The Lord is eternal and constant. The word "Jehovah" which is translated as "LORD" in Old Testament is constructed from the consonants of the name in Exodus and the vowels from another word meaning Lord. This combination was made to protect the holiness of the divine name. Greek has only one word for "Lord" and so we need to use the context to tell whether it is a title of politeness or allegiance.

The play on words that Jesus uses to argue with the Pharisees in **Matthew 22:41-46** makes the point that the descendant of David, who was the Messiah, must be greater than David or he would not call him "Lord". The Messiah is going to be more than an earthly ruler. He will hold spiritual authority too. In **Psalm 110** David declares that this king will also be a priest, and will be mightier than David. David's Lord will be a mighty warrior who will reign for ever. He sits at the right hand of God (ie higher than men and angels).

UNIT 26.3

WHY DO WE CALL JESUS "LORD"?

SESSION DATE: ☐☐☐

That the group members would understand that to call Jesus "Lord" means that we need to obey what He says, which includes serving each other.

LEADER'S CHECKLIST:

☐ Sketch & props (Part 1) ☐ Pens/Pencils/Paper

☐ Worksheets (Part 3) ☐ OHP/Visual Aid Board

☐ Lining paper/remote control car (Part 4) ☐ Bibles

☐ Illustrations (Part 5) ☐ Song Books

☐ Cardboard boxes (Part 6) ☐ Blutac

☐ Brainstorm sheet (Part 7) ☐ Notices

TEACHING CONTENT

TIME ALLOWANCE

1 THE USURPER 5-10

Perform the sketch as on the leaders' resource pages. Keep the pace fast and furious. The characters can be as daft as you like. Aim to make it part of a lively start to the session. Dressing in appropriate costume, even if it is only a cardboard crown and a curtain as a robe, will add to the fun of the sketch.

INPUT FROM LEADER
All the characters in the sketch called the king different things. Ask the group to list who called him what. The names they called him reflected their attitude towards him and their relationship with him. It also reflected their response to things he said. In this session we are going to be thinking about the title of Jesus that we use most often. As we will see, calling Jesus "Lord" has implications.

2. SPOT THE DIFFERENCE

5-10

Tell the group members to look up **Psalm 110:1** and compare it **Matthew 22:44**. They should soon notice that in the Psalm one of the words for "Lord" is written as "Lord".

> NOTE TO LEADER
> The passage in Matthew records a rather technical argument between Jesus and the Pharisees which most group members would find difficult to understand. It can be looked at in more detail in Digging Deeper. Try not to get bogged down with that argument here as you make the point about the need to obey Jesus.

INPUT FROM LEADER
The word "Lord" is used in the bible in a couple of ways. Sometimes it refers to God, and at other times it is a title similar to our word "Sir". It is easy to tell in the Old Testament which meaning is which, because when the word refers to God it is written as Lord in modern translations. When the word means "Sir", it is not written in capitals. In the New Testament we can't tell the difference very easily, because there is only one Greek word for "Lord". In this psalm, which King David wrote about 1,000 years before Jesus was born, he calls the Messiah "Lord". King David, who was the most important king in Israel's history, shows great respect for Jesus. We need to have the same respect as we use this title. That respect must lead to obeying Jesus' teaching.

3. BEARINGS

10-15

Give a copy of the worksheet to every group member, but allow them to work in pairs or teams if you think they will struggle on their own. The aim of the sheet is to show that wisdom, according to Jesus, is not assessed according to knowledge, but obedience.

> NOTE TO LEADER
> The answers to the quiz are: (1) A Sling; (2) Jonah; (3) Bethlehem; (4) 5 Loaves & 2 Fishes; (5) Martha & Mary; (6) Jordan; (7) Snake; (8) Timothy; (9) Fiery Furnace; (10) Peter; (11) Nazareth; (12) Wine; (13) Jesus; (14) Jerusalem; (15) Fig; (16) John; (17) Rome; (18) Crown of Thorns; (19) Joseph of Arimathea; (20) Babel.

INPUT FROM LEADER
Draw out the points at the bottom of the worksheet. We need to know what Jesus wants us to do by reading what He says in the bible. We must obey Him by putting it into practice. Link back to **Matthew 7:21**. Only those who do what God wants will enter heaven, not those who call Jesus "Lord".

4. AIR TRAFFIC CONTROLLER

15-20

Go into pairs for this activity. If the weather is fine, go outside for the activity. One person in the pairs is the air traffic controller, and the other person is the aeroplane. The aeroplane is blind-folded and guided around an obstacle course by the air traffic controller. Every time the plane hits an obstacle it loses a point, and when it has lost five points it is deemed to have crashed. Which plane can get the furthest?

> NOTE TO LEADER
> If you are cramped for room use this alternative. Set up a small course around which you can drive a remote control car. Adapt the input below, making the point that the car picks up the transmissions of the controller, and then obeys them. How pointless it would be if the car decided to only go and turn when it felt like it! Unlike the car, we have free choice. We can be obedient and wise, or disobedient and foolish.

INPUT FROM LEADER
The key to success in the activity is the aeroplane listening carefully to the instructions of the air traffic controller, and obeying them. Read through **Matthew 7:21-27**, focusing on verses 21 and 24. We need to know what the Father wants and what Jesus teaches. We must put it into practice. Calling Jesus "Lord" is not enough, we must obey Him.

5 MAKING MONEY `5-10`

Tell this story using the pictures on the leaders' resource pages. Cedric and Cynthia's school are trying to raise some money for Christian Aid. They decide that they are going to call at houses and offer to wash cars. Godfrey also reckons that car washing will bring in a lot of money, but he tells Ced & Cynth not to ask the people first. If you wash it and then tell the person they are bound to reward you, but if you ask first they may say they don't want it. Godfrey reckons he can make much more money on his own with his method than Ced and Cynth can make together. They agree to work on opposite sides of the same road. Ced and Cynth have to ask at five houses before they find someone who wants the car washed. Godfrey starts washing the first posh car he can find. When he's finished he goes to the door and tells the owner, who gets very angry saying "I never asked you". Godfrey protests saying "But sir, I've even scrubbed the wheel hubs", but the owner tells him to clear off. Ced and Cynth do a good job, and get duly rewarded.

INPUT FROM LEADER

Draw out the parallel between the story and **Matthew 7:21-23**. Godfrey did a good job, but he didn't do what the owner wanted. In fact he'd never bothered to find out. Calling the man "sir", and even doing something for him was of no use. Calling Jesus "Lord", and doing things we think He wants is not good enough. We need to know what Jesus wants by reading His teaching in the bible (verses 24-27), and then put it into practice. In that way we don't just call Him "Lord" but show that He really is in control of our lives.

6 MEMORY VERSE `10-15`

In pairs learn together **Matthew 7:21**. If you want to tie it in with the story of the house on the rock you could write the words on the side of cardboard boxes and then build them into a house. Take the bricks away one by one as you learn it.

7 THE CREEP `20-30`

Go into small groups and give each one the title "The Creep". The small groups should put together a short drama or mime that could carry that particular title. If possible ask each group to perform their pieces, but if you have a large group ask the small groups to perform their piece to just one other group. Remember that in exercises such as this it is the preparation of the drama rather than the performance of it is the most beneficial.

INPUT FROM LEADER

Draw out of the interpretations from the groups. Next, split the group into two halves and give those on the left hand side of the room **Matthew 25:31-33, 41-46** to read through. The right hand half of the room should read through **Matthew 25:31-40**. Writing the references on large card and displaying them on the appropriate side of the room would be helpful. Again, if you have a large group, adapt the activity by leaving the small groups in their pairing as above, splitting the readings between them. Ask the groups to say what the people in their half of the passage had, or had not done, for Jesus. Ask the group members to look at the other passage now. What do the two sets of people have in common? They both call the King "Lord". Link that back to **Matthew 7:21**. The people who were not allowed into the kingdom didn't realize that by serving and helping the King's subjects they would be helping the King himself. They were classic creeps - they were only nice to those they chose to be. They only chose to be nice when it would be of benefit to them. They didn't realize that when we help those in need, we are doing what God wants and serving Jesus Himself. We must not make the same mistake.

8 BRAINSTORM `10-15`

If you didn't use part 7, read through **Matthew 25:31-46**. If you did use that part, you could move straight into the brainstorm after giving the input above. Explain to the group that a brainstorm is a way of thinking of good ideas. People shout out their ideas, and then they are written up at the front without comment, no matter how impractical or silly they may seem. The key element of a brainstorm is that ridiculous and impractical suggestions often prompt someone else to think of a really good idea. Your brainstorm is all about how you can put into practice what Jesus is teaching in this story.

INPUT FROM LEADER
As the brainstorm begins, encourage it yourself by making some impractical suggestions such as "We could all go to Africa with a food parcel", etc. After you have filled up your piece of paper or acetate with suggestions, aim to move towards something practical you could do. Allow discussion at this stage. Make the point that not all the hungry and homeless live in Africa. Who in your parish can you help? In what way can you help them? Aim to finish this activity by getting the group to agree that the leaders should arrange something that will be of benefit to others in your community. Set yourself a small task, and then you are likely to achieve it (eg visiting some elderly people, or baking them some cakes, or making lonely members of the group feel welcome, etc.).

> NOTE TO LEADER
> You could point out that Jesus uses the title "Son of Man" about Himself at the beginning of this passage. Next session will be looking at what that title means.

9 SUMMARY

The title "Lord" is the one we use most of all when we are talking to Jesus. Using it doesn't guarantee a place in heaven. It is only when we live our lives with Jesus as Lord that we know we have a place in His Kingdom. We do this by obeying His teaching which involves serving each other.

10 DIGGING DEEPER

Use this part with a study or nurture group as well as making it a part of your own preparation. Look together at **Psalm 110:1** and the different places it is quoted in the New Testament. Build up a picture of the majesty of Jesus as you look at them.

Matthew 22:41-46 - Jesus uses Psalm 110 to turn the tables on the Pharisees who, having heard the Sadducees had failed to catch Him out, had tried to trick Him themselves. Read through the whole of Matthew 25. Although the Pharisees correctly stated that the Messiah was a descendant of David, they had failed to grasp the significance of David calling Him "Lord".

Acts 2:29-36 - What's the difference between David and Jesus?
1 Corinthians 15:25 - What is the ultimate enemy to be conquered?
Ephesians 1:20-23 - How extensive is Jesus' Lordship?
Hebrews 1:13 - In what way is Jesus seen as unique?
Hebrews 10:12-13 - What qualifies Jesus to sit at God's right hand?

FOR LEADERS ONLY

Is your teaching about the Lordship of Jesus consistent with your lifestyle? Young people remember the way we are years after they forget all we ever said.

THE USURPER

SCENE: KING AND QUEEN SAT ON THEIR THRONES WITH DUKE MARMADUKE OF MALMESBURY. THE ROYAL ADVISER IS STANDING TO ONE SIDE.

King: (SHOUTING REGALLY) Call the next subject.
Queen: Don't shout dearie.
King: (STILL SHOUTING) Pardon?
Queen: Don't shout dearie, you know it brings on one of my heads.
King: (ASIDE) Yes well any would be better than that one.
Queen: Pardon?
King: Nothing sweetness (TO MARMADUKE, DELIBERATELY WHISPERING) Could you call the next subject?
Duke: Yes your Superiorness (HE LOOKS AT A PIECE OF PAPER).
King: (TO QUEEN) I do like it when he calls me that, it adds a certain regality to everything.
Duke: The next subject will beeeee………Geography.
King: (CLIPPING HIM ROUND THE HEAD) Oh ha, ha, ha very witty. Not that sort of subject. Stop telling jokes and get on with it. Or perhaps you would like to be the court jester. Actually I think a little hat with bells on would quite suit you.
Duke: No, no, your munificence. I was merely trying to put some life into this otherwise dying sketch. No your Excellency, anything but the hat with bells on, your Graciousness.
King: OK get on with it.
Duke: Yes your Wonderfulness. The next subject is Crafty Casper Cuspince, wanted for treachery, treason and tree pinching (CASPER ENTERS THE ROOM AS IF HE HAS BEEN THROWN IN. HE KNEELS IN FRONT OF THE KING AND QUEEN).
King: So Cooper…
Duke: Casper!
King: Eh? Oh yes. So Casper we've caught you at last.
Casper: (STANDING UP) You may have me now but I shall soon be free, Egg Head.
King: Egg Head! How dare you call me Egg Head?! It's Egbert Corniche the 43rd to you.
Queen: Who is this horrible little man, Eggypoos?
King: Don't call me Eggypoos in front of the subjects dear. He's Kevin Cuprinol - some rogue or other.
Casper: Actually Queenie I'm Casper Cuspince, and soon I shall be King instead of this Eggypoos.
Duke: How dare you call His Marvellousness "Eggypoos". Say sorry at once.
Casper: Oh yeah, and who are you?
Duke: I'm Duke Marmaduke of Malmesbury. Adviser to his Kinglyness King Egbert Corniche the 43rd.
Casper: (PUSHES DUKE OVER) Creep.
King: Now look here, Cleethorpes.
Casper: Casper!
King: Oh all right, Casper. What is it you want you sniveling knave?
Casper: I want your throne Bertie.
King: Don't call me Bertie.
Queen: Anyway, don't be so silly, if you have the throne where will he sit?
Casper: Not the chair, the throne. I want to be King.
Queen: Oh that. Why didn't you say? We've been wanting to give up for a long time now haven't we dear? All this sitting around being called silly names, what sort of a job's that eh? Look you just give us time to get packed and then you can take over, how's that?
Casper: But, but, but…
King: Yes, that's right Jasper, you can take all this.
Casper: It's Casper.
King: Yes it probably is Cuthbert. (THE KING AND QUEEN EXIT QUITE HAPPILY).
Casper: Ha, it's all mine now (SITS ON THE THRONE). Now Malmy babes start treating me like the King or it's off with your head.
Duke: Oh shut up you wally (HE RUNS OFF).
Casper: Hey come back, come here all of you. Come and call me "King". Come and call me "Your majesty" (HE EXITS). Call me "Your excellence", somebody call me "Your highness"….

BEARINGS

HOW WISE ARE YOU?

Test out your wisdom by completing the twenty questions below.

1. David conquered Goliath using this weapon.
2. This man was in a fish for three days and nights.
3. The town where Jesus was born.
4. Jesus fed 5,000 people with this.
5. Two ladies whose brother Lazarus was raised from the dead by Jesus.
6. The river where John baptized.
7. This creature tricked Eve into committing the first sin.
8. Paul wrote two letters to this church leader.
9. Nebuchadnezzar threw three men into this hot place.
10. This disciple of Jesus had a name meaning "the rock".
11. Jesus grew up in this town.
12. Jesus said "Drink this in remembrance of Me"
13. John didn't want to baptize this person.
14. Jesus was crucified just outside the walls of this city.
15. This type of tree withered when Jesus cursed it.
16. This person wrote the fourth gospel.
17. The capital city of the Empire occupying Jerusalem in Jesus' time.
18. This was placed on Jesus' head just before He was crucified.
19. Jesus was buried in this person's tomb.
20. The place with a tower where languages were confused.

Your leader will check out your answers in a moment.

Most people think that being wise depends on how much we know. Jesus has a totally different way of assessing whether we are wise or not. Look up **Matthew 7:24-27** in your bibles.

What's the difference between a wise and foolish person according to Jesus?

What do you need to know, and what must you do if you are to be wise?

WHAT DOES "SON OF MAN" MEAN?

UNIT 26.4

BIBLE PASSAGES...

Daniel 7:11-14 (page 862 GNB)
Matthew 8:20 (page 12 GNB)
Matthew 17:12 & 22 (page 25 GNB)
Matthew 26:2,24,45 (pages 38-40 GNB)
Matthew 20:17-28 (page 29 GNB)
Matthew 24:23-31 (page 36 GNB)

FURTHER READING FOR LEADERS...

"**Matthew**" by RVG Tasker (IVP-Tyndale series) page 193f on the request about James and John.
"**The Lord is King**" by Ronald Wallace (IVP - Bible Speaks Today series) page 125f.

FOR GROUP MEMBERS...

"**The Bible from Scratch**" by Simon Jenkins (Lion) page 100.

DRAMA...

For sketches on the return of Jesus see COMPASS unit 18.4.

SONGS...

The suggestions in each session in this unit focus on who Jesus was. You could sing "You are the King of Glory" each week.
At your feet we fall **LP 10 / SF2 167 (28)**
God of Glory **LP 51 / SF2 197 (136)**
Hallelujah my Father **FS 6 / MP 66 / SF2 202 (149)**
His Name Is Wonderful **MP 72**
Jesus is King **LP 93 / SF2 236 (277)**
Jesus is Lord **MP 119 / SLW 82 / SF1 71 (278)**
Lord Jesus Christ **HF 58 (348) / LP 121**
Majesty **LP 123 / MP 151 / SF2 257 (358)**
You are the King of Glory **MP 279 / SF1 158 (630)**
You laid aside Your majesty **LP 230 / SF3 527 (638)**

Key:
- **FS** Fresh Sounds
- **HF** Hymns of Fellowship
- **LP** Let's Praise
- **MP** Mission / Pathfinder Praise
- **SF1/2/3** Songs of Fellowship 1/2/3
- **()** SF Integrated Music Edition
- **SLW** Sounds of Living Waters

PRAYER...

As you think about how you can follow Christ's example and serve each other, go into small groups and pray for each other.

CLUBNIGHT/PROJECT...

See under 26.1

GETTING READY...

We have learnt that "Messiah" was the title Jesus avoided using because it was so open to misinterpretation. The title "Son of Man" was clearly the preferred way that Jesus had of referring to Himself.

The Old Testament roots of the title lie in **Daniel 7:13-14**, which is unhelpfully translated "human being" in the GNB! This figure was clearly understood as someone who had eternal authority, and Jesus uses it particularly when referring to judgement and authority.

In Daniel's vision, the Son of Man is presented to God (13b). He is given authority, honour and royal power (14a). People of all nations, races and languages will serve Him (14a). His authority will last forever (14b). His kingdom will never end (14b). As you prepare, compare Daniel's vision with that of John in **Revelation 1:7-20**, paying special attention to verses 7, 13 and 18.

To the picture of eternal authority Jesus adds the dimension of suffering and service. Whilst maintaining the authority of the Son of Man, He demonstrates the way in which this works its way out.

This comes out clearly in the main passage in this session, which is **Matthew 20:20-28** when James and John had to learn the true nature of leadership. They, and their mother, had grasped the fact that Jesus was the "Son of Man" who would reign forever, but they had yet to learn the path of suffering that He must take. They also had to learn that following Christ would involve suffering. One of them was martyred and the other exiled.

As this session completes the unit, it is useful to summarize all that you have learnt together. This particular title of Jesus is the one that can be applied to us to a certain extent. We, too, are human and must follow our Lord in His pattern of service.

UNIT 26.4

WHAT DOES "SON OF MAN" MEAN?

SESSION DATE:

That the group members would understand that "Son of Man" was Jesus' favourite title because it helped people understand that He would suffer for their sake, yet one day reign forever.

LEADER'S CHECKLIST:

- [ ] Labels (Part 1)
- [ ] Scarf, hat, chocolate, knife, fork, die (Part 2)
- [ ] Index cards (Part 3)
- [ ] Worksheets (Part 4)
- [ ] Illustrations (Part 6)
- [ ] True/False cards (Part 7)
- [ ] Pens/Pencils/Paper
- [ ] OHP/Visual Aid Board
- [ ] Bibles
- [ ] Song Books
- [ ] Blutac
- [ ] Notices

TEACHING CONTENT

TIME ALLOWANCE

1 STAR CHOICE

10-15

Each group member needs to think of a favourite character whose name they write down on a sticky label, and wear. These characters could be historical, from the media, a cartoon character, etc. It doesn't matter what the group members like about the characters as long as they are happy to be identified with them. You may need to arbitrate between those who choose the same person. Next, play a name learning game such as shaking hands with everyone else in the group whilst seeking to remember the new names of the group members.

> NOTE TO LEADER
> The group members could keep these names right through the session if you are going to use part 8 as you summarize. The danger with this is that at a serious moment the adopted names may seem ridiculous and cause a break in concentration.

INPUT FROM LEADER
Remind the group of session 1 (part 4) in this unit when you learnt that Jesus did not like to use the title "Messiah" about Himself because of the misunderstanding it caused. The opposite is the case with the title "Son of Man". Jesus used more when talking about Himself than any other title. The reason for this was that it was less likely to cause confusion as the title "Messiah" would. In the same way as the group members were adopting the name of a favourite character, Jesus was taking on board the title of an Old Testament figure well known to the people in Israel. Look together at **Daniel 7:11-14**. The phrase "human being" is the same as "Son of Man", and is translated as such in versions other than the Good News Bible.

2 A MATTER OF TIME

15-20

Play this favourite with your group. If you have a large group you will need to split up into groups no larger than about six. The group members take it in turns to try to throw a six on a die, and then put on a scarf and hat and attempt to eat as much chocolate as possible, using a knife and fork, before the next person throws a six. You will need to make sure that no enterprising group member thinks of a way of bending the rules!

INPUT FROM LEADER
The activity has a very important time element to it. You only had the time from when you threw a six to when the next person threw one. You knew that your time would finish at some point, but you never knew when. The title "Son of Man" has its roots in the Old Testament. Look together at **Daniel 7:13-14**, reminding the group of the comments made about the phrase "human being" in the input for part 1, above. The title "Son of Man" is also a reminder that one day Jesus will come again. The character in Daniel's vision will reign forever one day. By calling Himself the Son of Man so often, Jesus makes it clear that it is He who will reign forever. We don't know how long we've got, as in the game, but we do know the end will come one day.

3 SUFFERING SERVANT

10-15

The title "Son of Man" occurs twenty-six times in Matthew's Gospel. On four occasions the verses talk about Jesus' authority. On thirteen occasions they talk about judgement and the second coming of Jesus. The other nine mentions of the title occur in eight different verses, and refer to Jesus suffering in some way. Write out one reference on each of eight index cards, and distribute them around the group. The group members need to look up the reference and write in their own words the way in which Jesus will suffer. The references are **Matthew 8:20; 17:12; 17:22; 20:18; 20:28; 26:2; 26:24; and 26:45**.

INPUT FROM LEADER
After the group members have finished, ask them to read out what they have written, one by one, and after each card has been read, stick it to the wall forming the shape of a cross. The title "Son of Man" points clearly to the fact that Jesus was became fully human even though He is the Son of God. He wasn't immune from pain, but would feel it in the same way as we would. Remind the group of what you have covered in this and the previous unit about Jesus' willingness to fulfil the will of His Father, and suffer that we might have our sins forgiven.

4 BEARINGS

10-15

Give a copy of the worksheet to every group member, but allow them to work in pairs or small groups if they want to. The answers are: (1) Cup of suffering; (2) Zebedee; (3) Fourth; (4) Revelation; (5) Destroy; (6) Sword; (7) Gethsemane; (8) Herod; (9) Jairus; (10) Boanerges; (11) Sons of Thunder; (12) Patmos; (13) Fishermen; (14) Peter; (15) Transfiguration.

INPUT FROM LEADER
Focus on the lesson that James and John had to learn by looking at **Matthew 20:25-28**. Leadership means service. Jesus as the "Son of Man" would be seen as this great leader who had authority over all things. Yet, He shows that He is the greatest servant of all by giving up even His life to redeem us.

MEMORY VERSE

10-15

Learn together **Matthew 20:27-28**. Do this by typing the verse out in capitals, and then cutting it up into individual words or phrases. Working on their own or in pairs, the group members must put the verses back together and then learn them.

THE COST OF RESPONSIBILITY

10-15

Tell this story using the illustrations on the leaders' resource pages or turn it into a piece of drama. Cedric is in a sulk because some of his class have been made prefects and he hasn't. Amongst others, his best friend Cecil has been chosen. What's worse, so has Cynthia! Now he's going to be bossed around by her...officially! At break he goes off to play football as usual and sees Cynthia on litter patrol on the playing field. It doesn't look much fun, he thinks. During the game he realizes that Cecil isn't there. Later on he finds out that Cecil was having to supervise the first years in the dinner queue. Cecil's new responsibilities mean that he'll only be able to play football a couple of times a week now. Being a prefect means having to give up. Being a leader means helping others and being a good example. Being a prefect, thinks Cedric, is not all it's made out to be!

INPUT FROM LEADER
We may think that having authority, or being in charge, is better than being bossed around. There are always responsibilities that go with leadership, though. Read through the story in **Matthew 20:20-28**. The two disciples in this story are James and John. They are not named here, but we know they are the sons of Zebedee. They are named in Mark's version of the story (chapter 10:35f). Focus on verses 25-28. All leadership carries responsibility, but Christian leadership means service. Jesus is our great example. He came not only to be a servant, but to sacrifice His life - the ultimate act of giving.

☐ NOTE TO LEADER
Use the additional input from the worksheets at this point if you omitted part 5.

SERVING GOD

15-20

Use the true and false cards on the leaders' resource pages as the basis for this activity on serving God. Additionally, you need a large piece of paper with a line down the middle and labeled "True" on one side, and "False" on the other. Go into groups of about five, or stay together if you are a small group. Distribute the cards around the group members. The first part of the activity is completed in silence with the group members putting down one of their statements on whichever side of the line they think is correct. They are also allowed to move one of the pieces of paper that have already been placed if they want to. Go around the group until all the cards have been placed, and then allow one final round in which the group members can move one card if they wish to.

INPUT FROM LEADER
This should be the first part of the exercise when discussion takes place. Ask the group members to talk about the activity, especially the cards that were moved about a lot. Tell them to look at **Matthew 20:25-26** and list the ways in which you can put this into practice in your own group. Contrast those suggestions with the kind of behaviour that happens at other groups the young people may belong to. What are the differences? Jesus makes it clear that we should be able to see the difference, and He - the Son of Man - is our great example as we seek to serve each other.

8. WHO DO YOU DO? `10-15`

Encourage some of the group members to do an impersonation of the characters they adopted for themselves in part 1. This could be in terms or voice, mannerisms, looks, or whatever. With some encouragement some of the more confident members of the group might be prepared to have a go. Alternatively, you could go into pairs and ask the group members to work out a "mirror" routine with their partner. They do this by pretending that they are on either side of a mirror, thus following each other's movements.

> **NOTE TO LEADER**
> Another alternative is for the group members to work on a "take-off" of a soap opera of some kind, and to impersonate the cast. Allow much more time for this.

INPUT FROM LEADER
Of the four titles of Jesus we have looked at in this unit, "Son of Man" is the only one that we can follow as our example. None of us can be the "Messiah", or the "Son of God" in the unique way that Jesus was, or the "Lord". Each of us is human though, and we can follow the example of Jesus. He is the one we need to work hard on impersonating every day of our lives. So often we like to stick to our "rights", to what we think we deserve. Jesus, though, gave up everything in order that we might be redeemed, or bought back for God. Finish by looking back to the few verses that occur just before the passage we concentrated on in this session - **Matthew 20:17-19**. Encourage a short time of silence or prayer before moving on to summarize the session.

9. SUMMARY

Jesus used the title "Son of Man" about Himself, as it emphasized His humanity, and linked Him to the Old Testament prophecies about the figure who had eternal authority. Jesus suffered and died as a man, but was raised to life. That was when His true authority was revealed. He has been given everlasting authority, though, and one day He will return to earth again bringing judgement and salvation.

10. DIGGING DEEPER

Use this part with a study or nurture group as well as making it a part of your own preparation. Look together at **Matthew 24:23-31**. This passage focuses on the rôle of the return of Jesus as judge. The title "Son of Man" refers to the return of Jesus in half the occasions it is used in this gospel.

a Can you think of any people who could be called "false Messiahs"?
b Why is Jesus telling people this?
c How quickly will this event happen?
d What do you think verse 28 means?
e Why will people weep when The Son of Man appears?
f What hope do His people have in the face of this terrifying prophecy?
g What can we do to be ready?

FOR LEADERS ONLY

As leaders, do we fulfil the rôle of the "servants of the rest"?

TRUE OR FALSE

God doesn't want us to suffer when we serve Him	Passing Exams has nothing to do with serving God
If you're being paid, you can't be serving God	Preaching is the best way of serving God
It's easier to serve God than your parents	Ringing the church bells is serving God
It's harder to serve God at home than at church	Serving God may be painful
Looking properly after your budgie is serving God	The only way to serve God is to be the Vicar
Men serve God better than women	We should only serve God on Sundays
Only certain people can serve God	You cannot serve God at School

LEADERS' RESOURCE PAGES

BEARINGS

FAX ON JAMES & JOHN

Fill your answers in the boxes below, looking up the references if you need to. Look down the marked column in order to find the answer to the question at the bottom.

1   Jesus asked if they could drink from this (**Matthew 20:22**)
2   This was the name of their father (**Matthew 4:21**)
3   This numbered gospel was written by one of these brothers
4   This book, written by John, includes a vision about Jesus
5   They wanted to do this to a Samaritan village (**Luke 9:54**)
6   James was put to death in this way (**Acts 12:2**)
7   They went with Jesus to pray in this garden (**Matthew 26:36-37**)
8   The name of the person who ordered the death of James (**Acts 12:2**)
9   They witnessed Jesus raise this man's daughter from the dead (**Mark 5:37-38**)
10 They were given this nickname (**Mark 3:17**)
11 The meaning of the nickname (**Mark 3:17**)
12 The island where John was exiled (**Revelation 1:9**)
13 This was their occupation (**Matthew 4:21**)
14 They spent a lot of time with this person and Jesus (**Mark 5:37; 9:2; 14:33**)
15 They were witnesses of this spectacular event (**Matthew 17:1**)

What does Jesus say that we must do? (Look at the marked column)